'As
To be purs
everlasting life, and, for a
enormous dimensions'

 – E. V. Lucas, speaking of his
  black Spaniel, Shadow

'All knowledge, the totality of all
questions and all answers, is contained
in the dog'

 – Franz Kafka

'People are inclined to sneer if one claims
that dogs can understand nearly every
word we say . . . In fact they can understand
every thought let alone words, for they
have an acute telepathic sense and the
spoken word becomes unnecessary'

 – Barbara Woodhouse

MELISSA MILLER'S DEFINITIVE I.Q. TEST FOR DOGS AND I.Q. TEST FOR DOG OWNERS

A SIGNET BOOK

SIGNET

Published by the Penguin Group
Penguin Books Ltd, 27 Wrights Lane, London w8 5tz, England
Penguin Books USA Inc., 375 Hudson Street, New York, New York 10014, USA
Penguin Books Australia Ltd, Ringwood, Victoria, Australia
Penguin Books Canada Ltd, 10 Alcorn Avenue, Toronto, Ontario, Canada m4v 3b2
Penguin Books (NZ) Ltd, 182–190 Wairau Road, Auckland 10, New Zealand

First published 1993
1 3 5 7 9 10 8 6 4 2

Typeset by Datix International Limited, Bungay, Suffolk
Printed in England by Clays Ltd, St Ives plc
Set in 10.5/13 pt Monophoto Sabon

In fond memory of my grandparents,
who did so much for the welfare of dogs,
and of Cinnamon, a Chow Chow

CONTENTS

ACKNOWLEDGEMENTS

I would like to thank Mary Ann Naples for encouraging me to pursue this idea, and Peter Carson for giving me the chance to write another fun pet book. Thanks are also due to Abner Stein and his gang for their support and assistance, to Celia Haddon for lending me so many dog books, to Pamela Friedmann for sending me numerous articles on dogs, to Marti Leimbach for her reference suggestions, and to Mary Omond for her excellent and thorough editing.

My thanks to the staff at the Elizabeth Street Veterinary Clinic in London, who helped me to find dogs to test as part of my research, and to all the dog owners who voluntarily tested their dog's I.Q. and sent me their scores and very useful comments.

I am also deeply grateful to Alexander Jones for his generous flexibility with my work schedule, and to Julian Burney for his support, editorial assistance and patience.

For their permission to quote from copyright material, I would like to thank the following: A. & C. Black (Publishers) Ltd, for quotes from *Dogs, Their History and Development* (vols 1 and 2) by Edward C. Ash (copyright 1927 by Edward C. Ash); the *Boston Globe* for a quote from their 23 January 1993 article 'Cats Chase Dogs off the No. 1 Spot'; Dorling Kindersley Ltd for a quote from *The Ultimate Dog Book* by David Taylor (copyright © David Taylor, 1990); the *Evening Standard* for quotations from their 4 May 1993 article 'Miracle Worker Dogs Give Patients a New Lease of Life'; HarperCollins, London, and Avv. Maria Teresa de Simone Niguesa, for a quote from *The Baron in the Trees* by Italo Calvino (copyright © Italo Calvino, 1959); Clifford L. B. Hubbard, Ponterwyd, Wales, for an extract from his book *An Introduction to the Literature of British Dogs* (copyright 1949 by Clifford L. B. Hubbard); Judy Publishing Co., Chicago, for quotes from *Dog Scrap Book and Anthology* by Will Judy (copyright © Will Judy, 1958); McIntosh and Otis Inc., New York, for a quotation from an essay by John Steinbeck entitled 'Random Thoughts on Random Dogs', in the *Saturday Review*, 8 October 1955 (copyright © John Steinbeck, 1955, copyright © Elaine and Thom Steinbeck, and John Steinbeck IV, 1983); Frederick Muller Ltd for extracts from *In Praise of Dogs* by G. L. Stampa (copyright 1948 by G. L. Stampa); Harold Ober Associates, New York, for quotes from *Every Dog Should Have a Man* (copyright 1952 by Corey Ford); Octopus Publishing Group for extracts from *The Treasury of Dogs* (copyright © Barbara Woodhouse and Wendy Boorer, 1972); Pelham Books Ltd for quotes from *The Dog's Mind* by Bruce Fogle (copyright © Bruce Fogle, 1990) and for quotes from *Animal Heroes* by Yvonne Roberts (copyright © Yvonne Roberts, 1990); Ringpress Books Ltd for quotes from *How Your Dog Thinks* by Barbara Woodhouse (copyright © Barbara Woodhouse, 1992); Robson Books Ltd for quotes from *Dogs' Tales* by June Whitfield (copyright © June Whitfield, 1987); Simon & Schuster, New Jersey, for a quotation from *Cold Noses and Warm Hearts*, preface by Corey Ford (copyright © Corey Ford, 1958, 1986); Stanmore Press Ltd for an extract from *Just Dogs and Things* by Honor Green (copyright © Honor Green, 1964).

I regret that, despite every effort, I have been unable to reach the copyright holders of an extract from the *The Bunch Book* by James Douglas; a quote from *Dogwatching* by Desmond Morris, Jonathan Cape, 1986; and selected quotes from the *Page-a-Day Dog Calendar*, Workman Publishing Co., New York. I also regret that I have not been able to find the copyright holders of quotes from *The Practical Dog Book* by Edward C. Ash, 1931; a translated quote from *La Vie Intime* attributed to Wilhelmina Swainston-Goodger's *The Pug Dog, Its History and Origin*, 1930; and a quote from *Just a Mutt* by Eldon Roark, 1947. Should the copyright holders contact the publisher, acknowledgement will be made in future printings.

I
INTRODUCTION

*All knowledge, the totality of all questions and all answers,
is contained in the dog.*

· Franz Kafka (1883–1924) ·

———————

O F ALL ANIMALS in the world, the dog has afforded
mankind the greatest benefits through its intelligence and
its nature. Blessed with an outstanding memory, five extraordinary senses (possibly six), as well as an ability to reason,
the dog's superb mental faculties are coupled with a virtuous
character and a remarkable eagerness to please its owner,
making it the most versatile and rewarding animal that man
has known.

Dogs were the first animals to settle with us and have been
at our side for over six thousand years, demonstrating time
and again that they are fully capable of assuming the ever-
increasing roles we assign to them. The oldest roles are that of
assistant hunter and guard. Indeed, the relationship between
man and dog began as a trade-off between the dog's superior
ability to see, hear and chase prey, and to detect advancing
predators early on, and man's provision of a relatively stable
food supply and shelter; the dog was instrumental in man's
progression from a nomadic hunting lifestyle to a more settled
existence, once man learned how to train it to manage herds
and flocks of animals.

Dogs soon took on the role of companion and pet too, and
by about 4000 BC in Ancient Egypt were revered and valued
as such. Over time, they were variously bred and trained to
become entertainers, workers, trackers and haulers, and more
recently as rescuers, guides for the physically impaired, friends
to the lonely, film stars and even astronauts!

Yet the average pet dog, which is not highly trained for any
specific role, can be quite clever in its own way too. Most
dogs, for example, have an excellent memory, which some
people believe surpasses our own; they can recognize quite

easily the particular sound of food being placed in their bowls and, more impressively, remember where they buried something several years ago, even if they haven't been back to that spot since.

Many of the dog's memories are related to its sense of smell which enables it, for instance, to recognize a person it may have met only once before. The dog's sense of smell is the most powerful of any animal other than the eel. Some dogs can detect changes in the scent of a substance which are as small as one part per million.

This phenomenal ability enables the dog to sense changes in our moods and emotions, because these affect our own particular scent. Extremely perceptive animals, dogs are further able to understand how we are feeling and 'know' what we are thinking by watching our body language. Our intentional attempts to communicate with them are usually well-received too. Most dogs have a keen desire to understand their owner, and their sensitive hearing ability enables them to differentiate between our various tones and sounds to perceive the meaning of many of our words.

Dogs are able to interpret and respond to their environment intelligently in ways we don't always fully understand. Like cats and horses, they are able to anticipate an imminent storm or earthquake, and many dogs also have the mysterious ability to find their way home if they are lost, sometimes over many hundreds and even thousands of miles!

Moreover, and contrary to what some people claim, it is my firm belief that most dogs also possess an ability to reason. The best evidence can be seen in the many stories about dogs who, faced with an emergency or a crisis, were able to respond quickly and appropriately, sometimes saving the lives of men; such dogs were able to think independently and creatively, without the benefit of any previous training or stored knowledge of how to act in such a situation. On these occasions, man is indebted to the dog's fine character as well as to its intelligence; few other animals would put their lives at risk with no hesitation.

Given the different ways a dog can demonstrate its intelligence, how does one go about measuring it? Trying to assess the intelligence of animals is tricky because they aren't able to express themselves in speech, at least not to any significant extent, so one must look instead to their behaviour and their responses to certain situations for clues about their intelligence. The Definitive Dog I.Q. Test which follows is based loosely on I.Q. tests for humans and measures six of the seven areas of mental ability that human tests measure. These are memory (your dog's response when you bring out its lead), perception (ability to detect your moods), vocabulary (breadth of dog sounds), verbal apprehension (your dog's response when its name is called), spatial ability (judging the speed and distance of a thrown object) and reasoning ability (how to procure extra food). The test also assesses related mental areas such as imagination, curiosity, communication skills and, of course, training. Several questions refer to your dog's personality as it also reflects its level of intelligence.

The test is meant to be accurate but, above all, entertaining and amusing to take. Owners answer the questions on behalf of their dog, drawing largely upon past observations of behaviour. The dog does need to be present for some of the questions which test its spontaneous reaction to certain stimuli and situations. The questions are grouped into four areas: visual skills, audio skills, social behaviour and domestic behaviour. When you refer to the scoring table at the end of the test, you will see that some questions have two answers which are awarded the same number of points, that there are sometimes two 'smartest' or 'dumbest' answers to the same question. This is intentional since different breeds may respond differently to the same situation and dogs have different personalities. A loud, active dog may be just as clever as a quiet, sedentary one.

After adding up your dog's score, you should refer to the Dog I.Q. Conversion Graph within the results section to convert the score to a Dog I.Q. The average I.Q. for dogs is equal to 100, as it is in I.Q. tests for humans. This has been determined from the average score of a representative sample of domestic dogs (and one police dog), each of which was tested by its owner using this test; the dogs and their owners are named in the Sample Pool of Domestic Dogs: List of Participants. Your dog's I.Q. can be measured against this sample of the domestic dog population to determine whether it is Blissfully Ignorant, Generally Thick, Occasionally Clever, Average, Brighter Than Average, Very Intelligent, Extremely Intelligent or a Canine Genius. (As an additional benchmark, it may interest you that the highly trained police dog did indeed have the top score of the sample group, ranking in the Canine Genius category.)

But how high is your own I.Q. as a dog owner? Dogs naturally assume a subservient role to their owners whom they instinctively consider to be their 'pack leader'. Your intelligence as an owner is therefore more important than the intelligence of your dog in determining the success of your relationship.

The Definitive Dog Owner I.Q. Test gives you a chance to measure your knowledge of the responsibilities of dog ownership, and your willingness to accept them, your sensitivity and attitude towards your dog, and your efforts in the relationship. As in the I.Q. Test for Dogs, there is a greater emphasis on entertainment than on accuracy, but the test may offer you new insights into your relationship with your dog. After a few background questions which examine your past experience with dogs, the test is divided into three further sections to assess your dedication, sensitivity and success in training your dog – as well as your dog's success in 'training' you!

Once you have finished the test and added up all your points, you can refer to the results section to convert your score to a Dog Owner I.Q. You should then consult the Dog Owner I.Q. Classification Table to determine what type of owner you are. The highest scoring category is that of the Sensible Owner who has an intelligent and well-balanced view of dog ownership; Sensible Owners consider training to be important but attention and care even more so. The second highest category is the Doting Owner. Extremely dedicated to their dog and highly sensitive to its needs, the only fault of some Doting Owners is that they consider training less important than it should be – and sometimes they don't consider it at all. In the next category, Congenial Owners tend to be more relaxed in their relationship with their dog, providing for it perfectly well but without lavishing attention on it or putting too much emphasis on training. The fourth and lowest-scoring category is that of the Demanding Owner who insists on a well-behaved dog but who should give it a little more attention. Detailed descriptions of owner types and recommended dog breeds for each are included after the test.

Following the test is a chapter entitled 'The Rewards of Dog Ownership', which highlights some of the benefits of owning a dog. It also points out certain attributes of the dog which many of us would do well to recognize and emulate. Although we try to teach dogs certain tricks and standards of behaviour, almost all of us could learn a thing or two from them! A dog can be a daily reminder of how to live life fully, honestly and cheerfully.

At the end of the book is a one-page questionnaire which asks for the I.Q.s of both yourself and your dog, as well as other relevant information such as your dog's breed and age, the number of years you have kept a dog, and any 'Blissfully Ignorant' or 'Canine Genius' stories you may have about your dog. I am collecting this data for a follow-up analysis of the I.Q.s of dogs and their owners; if you would like to contribute to the research, I would be most grateful.

As you take the tests, have fun and remember that the results shouldn't be taken too seriously! Your I.Q. as an owner is more important than the I.Q. of your dog because of your leading role in the relationship. An owner's responsibilities extend beyond the provision of food and an annual trip to the vet. They also include emotional support, a sensitivity to your dog's behaviour and body language, and at least a little training since all dogs gain satisfaction from pleasing their owners. Those who accept these responsibilities are much more likely to have happy, well-adjusted and intelligent dogs that are rewarding to keep.

II
THE INTELLIGENT DOG

*Men cannot think like dogs . . . [there exists] a sharp difference
in the mental capacity of humans and canines. For example,
a human who is given an intricate problem will spend all day
trying to solve it, but a canine will have the sense to give up
and do something else instead.*

· Corey Ford, *Every Dog Should Have a Man* ·

THE DOG HAS a more impressive capacity for intellectual
thought than it is often given credit for. Born with a large
genetic pool of instinctive thinking patterns inherited from its
ancient ancestors, the wolves, its intelligence is enhanced by a
well-developed brain very similar to our own, superb physical
senses and a strong ability and willingness to learn.

Dogs demonstrate their high level of intelligence in a number
of ways. With their outstanding memory (which some say is
better than our own), dogs can be trained to suppress even the
strongest of natural instincts. But they can also reason and
think for themselves as seen most dramatically when they save
lives, determining in an instant the best response to a crisis.
Acutely sensitive to changes in their environment, including
not only those in the atmosphere but in our own expressions
and moods as well, dogs have also earned a reputation for
telepathic thought. Although many questions remain about
the possibility of a sixth sense in dogs, what we do know
about their five other senses, and their ability to think, is quite
remarkable.

THE INTELLIGENT DOG'S BRAIN AND
SENSORY SKILLS

Intelligence is often defined as an ability to comprehend meaning or a capacity to understand; this is directly related to an
animal's cognitive power – its ability to perceive and interpret

the signals it receives from its environment. In this respect the dog is very well-equipped.

The Brain

The dog's brain is a complex and extremely active organ which demands over 20 per cent of the animal's blood supply. Like our brain, it has three major parts: the largest section, the cerebrum, which controls learning, emotions and behaviour; a smaller section, the cerebellum, controlling muscles; and the stem, connecting the brain to the rest of the body's nervous system.

As far as most dog owners are concerned, one of the most important parts of the dog's brain is its limbic system. This controls the dog's memory and its level of interest and is therefore instrumental in the dog's ability to be trained. 'If the reward we are offering [in training] is less rewarding than what the dog is engaged in, it is in the limbic system that he "decides" not to obey a command,' says veterinarian Bruce Fogle.

Perhaps the most important point for humans to remember about the dog's brain is that its functionality and even its size can be increased through greater sensory stimulation; more interaction with other animals and people, more games or toys to play with, new environments and changes of scene to explore – all will stimulate the dog's brain and make it more efficient and powerful.

The Five Senses

Of all of the dog's senses which it uses to great effect in understanding its environment, the most important is its sense of smell. A dog can literally 'read' its environment with its nose. Though different breeds have different levels of ability, dogs are generally so much better than we are at detecting scents that it is sometimes hard to fathom!

For example, some dogs can distinguish two smells which differ by only one part per million. In our less powerful nose, we have approximately five specialized 'smell receptors' for every 220 in the average dog's. The sensitive membrane lining inside a dog's nose has a greater surface area than that of the dog's entire body – seven square metres on average compared with our half metre.

Men have no sense of smell.
All the average man uses his nose for is to keep his glasses on.

· Corey Ford ·

Many experiments confirm the dog's powerful sense of smell. In one test six men were each given a pebble which they held only momentarily and then threw as far as they were able; one of the men then let the test dog smell his hand, and the dog proceeded to find and bring back the pebble which *he* had thrown. In another experiment a set of glass plates was used where only one of the plates was touched just once by a person's fingertip. The plates were then stored for six weeks but the dog being tested was able to detect which plate had been touched even then!

Man has made use of this tremendous ability in dogs in many ways. The U.S. Department of Agriculture employs a 'Beagle Brigade' to sniff out drugs at airports. The U.S. Army uses their scent-tracking abilities to detect hidden mines and explosives. It has concluded that no animal (and they tested many), machine or scientific instrument exists that can beat a dog's nose for their purposes.

Some dogs have been bred specifically for their scenting abilities, such as Bloodhounds which are often used to track criminals and to hunt. Following ground scents, Bloodhounds can detect the smell of a human foot up to four days after the scent has been laid, and they can track a smell for a hundred miles. Border Collies are outstanding at picking up scents in the air and are also chosen by search and rescue teams. St Bernards are particularly good at finding people trapped underneath snow, and it has recently been discovered that they have infra-red detectors inside their nose, allowing them to detect whether the person buried by snow is alive or not.

Dogs use their sense of smell in their relationships with us too. Memories of a scent stay with dogs for life, allowing them not only to recognize us by our own particular scent, but also to detect shifts in our moods and attitudes by the subsequent changes in our body odour.

The dog's sense of hearing is also superior to ours. As with its sense of smell, hearing was critically important to the dog's ability to hunt and survive when it lived in the wild, and this strong ability to hear has been passed on to the domestic dog. It can hear sounds at four times the distance we can, and is able to differentiate between two notes that are just one eighth of a tone apart. Dogs can also hear ultrasonic sounds which are too high for us to pick up.

Some dogs are able to move their ears to 'tune in' to a sound and hear it more accurately. The Akita and German Shepherd, for instance, are particularly good at using just one ear to determine where a sound is coming from, then listening to it with both ears to capture all the sound waves.

Sight in dogs varies among breeds and is better than man's in some but not all respects. Dogs are more sensitive than we are to movement and light but less skilled at picking up detail. 'If a dog's owner remains motionless at a distance of 300 yards the animal cannot detect him,' writes Desmond Morris in *Dogwatching*. 'If, on the other hand, a shepherd is one mile distant but making bold hand signals, these can be clearly seen by his sheepdog,' he continues. This explains why so many of the species wild dogs preyed upon will immediately freeze when they think they've been spotted by a predator.

Dogs have a wider field of vision than we do. In contrast to our 180 degrees, dog breeds with narrow heads and lateral eyes, such as setters, can see a 270-degree spectrum, though flat-faced breeds with frontal eyes see less. What they gain in wide angular vision, however, is offset by their relatively poor binocular vision; most dogs are less adept at focusing on objects close up and on perceiving depth of field than we are.

Like cats, dogs can also see in much dimmer light than we can. At the back of their eyes is a layer of light-reflecting cells which allows them to intensify the limited amount of light available. Dogs, though, are not as well-equipped as cats are as they only have one layer of these cells compared with the cat's fifteen.

The fourth sense, touch, is vitally important to the development of a mature mind in the dog. In training it is the most powerful reward a dog can receive, even more than food. It is as critical to a dog's emotional well-being as it is to ours. Dogs also use their sense of touch to explore and understand their environment. They are equipped with special hairs under their jaws, on their muzzles and eyebrows which can detect air currents, as well as an object's texture or shape.

The fifth sense, taste, is the least important to dogs. Here we really excel with our 9,000 taste buds compared with the dog's 1,700 or so. Dogs can sense sweet, salty and sour or bitter tastes, but not nearly as well as we can. Much more important to a dog is the smell of its food, followed by the food's texture, then its taste.

Lastly, although it isn't one of the five physical senses, the dog's internal sense of time should be mentioned. Many dogs have an extremely accurate body clock which they use to their own and sometimes to their owner's benefit. Farmers, for instance, often rely on their dogs to wake them up. One in America is woken at 5.59 a.m. precisely by his collie; the collie must rely on his internal body clock as any clock would strike on the hour at 6 a.m., not the minute before. The only drawback, according to the farmer, is that his dog does the same thing on Sundays when he *could* sleep in. But another American was able to train his dog to fetch the morning paper and wake him up every day *except* Sundays, when the dog would know not to bother.

THE INTELLIGENT DOG'S ABILITY TO THINK

The dog has an enviable mind;
it remembers the nice things in life
and quickly blots out the nasty.

· Barbara Woodhouse ·

It isn't hard to refute the idea that dogs are stupid. Many people mistake some of the dog's instinctive behaviour patterns as 'dumb' or misread their dog's keen desire to please as an inability to learn from experience or to discriminate and reason.

For instance, watching a dog voluntarily roll itself in rubbish or in another dog's droppings certainly doesn't look like intelligent behaviour to the untrained eye. But this instinct is something almost all dogs inherited from their predatory days when it was very clever indeed to mask their own body odour with a stronger one.

Digging holes for no apparent purpose is another of the dog's seemingly pointless activities. But, again, dogs in the wild would dig to look for prey such as rodents or at other times to store food or bones for a rainy day. Today's domestic dog doesn't usually have such motives but will enjoy digging anyway because it 'feels' right and because of the tempting array of organic smells it discovers in the ground.

Another example of apparently 'dumb' behaviour is cited by the American dog lover, Will Judy, in his poem 'Dumb Dog, Dumb Dog, Dumb Dog!':

> . . . He feign would drop to slumber deep and sound
> But you, your smallest move, he needs must watch.
> Down in the cool and quiet cellar, bed is kept for him –
> Yet by your side in hot and stifling room, he gasps content.
> DUMB DOG, DUMB DOG, DUMB DOG!

It is my belief that as with most dogs, this one *would* have chosen to sleep in the cool cellar had it not been so important to it to please and be loved by its master. The distinction between a dog's seemingly stupid but loving behaviour and a dog's inability to think should be made.

Will Judy considered the dog's chief mental attributes to be both pride and humility, a great imagination, an ability to identify property, and a sense of right and wrong which he believed to be related to its most important mental attribute, memory. He didn't, however, believe that dogs could reason: '[Dogs] do not conclude an entirely new idea from what they already know . . . the dog acts mostly out of imitation, out of remembrance, out of accident, which in turn is remembered and repeated.'

The story of a Chow Chow, in London illustrates this level of intelligence. The Chow lived very close to a park and used to go for walks there by himself. One day he happened to sit down at the park's taxi rank; one of the drivers spotted him, presumed he was lost and approached him to read the tag on his collar. The driver then took the Chow home and was paid by the dog's owner.

The Chow remembered this accidental but pleasing episode and soon it became a regular occurrence. 'The taxi-men all [recognized] a potential customer,' writes Honor Green. 'One of the wags on the rank used to get out, open his taxi's door, saying, "Taxi, sir?" whereupon the Chow would nonchalantly get in, step up on to the seat, [and] lean back against the cushions, almost saying, "Drive on, my good fellow!"'

Although this is a light-hearted example, there is no denying that the memory of dogs is very impressive and has been greatly admired by man for thousands of years. In the Ancient Greek epic, the *Odyssey*, for instance, the Greek warrior Ulysses spends eight years in the Trojan War before returning home (in a dog's life span the equivalent of fifty human years). Ulysses was able to disguise himself from his unfaithful wife and household, but not from his dog, Argus, who jumped for joy as soon as he saw him.

[Men] cannot recall where they put something, like the nozzle of the garden hose or the keys to the car. A dog can find a bone he buried three years ago, but a man will spend half a day hunting in the closet for his old fishing hat, and then have to shout downstairs and ask his wife where she hid it.

· Cory Ford ·

Related to the dog's memory is its ability to understand what we say, though there is some debate as to whether it does this by recognizing just the tones we use or if it actually understands our words. The story of a dog named 'Flip' might lead us to believe that dogs *can* understand our words. Flip, a mongrel, accompanied his owner's young daughters to dance class one day, about ten blocks from their house. But Flip made a nuisance of himself so the daughters called home for help. 'Put Flip on the phone,' their mother demanded. 'Flip, you're in the way over there ... You come straight home!'

Looking slightly embarrassed, Flip quietly crept towards the door and went home immediately.

———————

I believe that by being constantly with their owners, by listening to conversation, and by connecting certain sounds with certain actions, the dog can and does understand about 400 words, more if it is a well-loved, extremely intelligent dog.

· Barbara Woodhouse ·

———————

Many dogs draw upon their excellent memories and related abilities such as verbal apprehension to help them to reason and solve problems, contrary to what Will Judy and others believe. Consider the example of Sweep, an obedient spaniel. His master habitually took off Sweep's collar at the end of the day and put it on a low table within Sweep's reach. Every morning Sweep used to take his collar in his mouth and bring it to his master, ready for a walk, but one morning he arrived without it. When his master told him, 'Collar! Go fetch it,' Sweep disappeared for quite a while before returning with one of his master's *shirt* collars in his mouth.

Writes the storyteller: 'Clearly, when Sweep found that his collar was not in its accustomed place, he must have reasoned something like this: He took it off last night and, I expect, absentmindedly put it in his pocket. He didn't say to me just now, "Bring *your* collar." He said, "Collar! Fetch it." Afterwards [the master] found the dog's collar in the game pocket of his tweeds.'

With regard to the dog's ability to think, there has also been some debate as to whether pedigree dogs are brighter than mongrels. Some people believe that pedigrees are generally cleverer because they are more refined or because intelligence can be enhanced through breeding. But many others believe that mongrels are brighter, inheriting certain 'street-smarts' that pure-bred dogs don't have access to. In fact, a dog's intelligence is more profoundly affected by its training and contact with people than it is by any instinctive knowledge.

THE INTELLIGENT DOG AS HERO

The strongest illustration of a dog's ability to think and to reason is when it is faced with a completely new situation for which it has no relevant memories to draw upon, and it has to determine the possible solutions to the problem, weigh the merits of one against another, and act 'correctly' and intelligently. There are many such stories recorded in the history of dogs, the most impressive being acts of heroism.

A dog in Texas, for instance, was thrown from his owners' car when it had a blow-out on the highway and the car rolled down an embankment. It then started to catch fire, with the dog's owners still inside, unconscious. The dog raced up to the highway and barked furiously at every car that passed until a driver stopped. The dog led the stranger down the slope to the car and the couple were saved.

A remarkable ability to sense danger and respond quickly was demonstrated by a setter named Irish in New Jersey. It was Irish's habit to lie in front of the shop run by his master and watch the pedestrians and cars go by. One day he saw a small child wander away from his mother, who was busy shopping, and watched as the child toddled into the street. A few people also spotted the boy and gasped as they saw the approaching cars, but Irish didn't lose a moment. Darting out and getting hold of the child's trousers, Irish was able to pull him back to the pavement.

The National Humane Association awarded a life-saving medal in 1941 to Poochie, a white mongrel from Illinois, for his gallantry and ability to improvise, which saved not only his master's life but the lives of several others as well. His owner, Robert 'Bubber' Jones, had taken a friend and Poochie to the Mississippi River one day for a swim. Upon their arrival, they could hear screams for help; some boys were in danger of drowning in a fierce undercurrent. Poochie, Jones and their friend raced in to help, each grabbing a boy. On their third rescue, Jones became exhausted and Poochie swam over so that Jones could grab hold of his tail. Poochie carried on swimming despite the 130-pound weight difference. With Jones floating – and breathing – in tow, Poochie was able to bring him ashore.

THE INTELLIGENT DOG IN
TRAINING

Another way that man has benefited from the intelligence of dogs is through the remarkable willingness and ability of many breeds to be trained. Using their memory primarily, dogs learn through repetition to associate 'good' behaviour with pleasing rewards such as praise, love or food and 'bad' behaviour with less desirable consequences. The dog's eagerness to please is also important in training, something heavily influenced by the respect it has for the person trying to train it.

One of the most difficult things a dog in training must learn is to overcome certain instinctive behaviour patterns, such as the submissive action of rolling on to its back with its legs in the air or doing its business inside. Instinctive behaviours are deep-seated and often difficult to change, but through thoughtful training many dogs can be taught to behave differently. Sheepdogs, for instance, can learn to drive a flock *away* from their master (the pack leader), the exact opposite of what they'd instinctively do.

On the other hand some of the most productive training methods capitalize on particular instincts a dog may have. 'Wherever possible we use the dog's natural instincts if they can be guided into the right channels,' writes Barbara Woodhouse. For example, when teaching a dog to track, placing food at the end of a trail is a terrific incentive to those breeds whose natural instinct is to use their nose to find food. Another example is the retriever who, naturally eager to bring food back to its basket, is encouraged to do so when training for a hunt.

One of the most impressive illustrations of a well-trained dog is the guide dog for the blind, which is intelligent enough to be taught a number of different lessons and behaviours, little of which can truly be called instinctive. The Guide Dogs for the

Blind Association runs the largest dog breeding programme in the world, choosing Labrador or Golden Retriever crosses, and some Alsatians and Collies, for their stamina, size and disposition. In the training programme a puppy will spend its first year with a volunteer family who introduces it to shops, traffic and crowds, as well as to elementary commands. 'The dogs are then returned to the Association,' writes Yvonne Roberts in *Animal Heroes*, '[where] they are taught how to be "intelligently disobedient" – for example, disregarding a command to cross a road when a car is coming ... and also to think of themselves as being about six feet tall and four feet wide, in order to negotiate obstacles like low branches and scaffolding for themselves and their owners.'

More recently dogs have also been trained as hearing aids for the deaf. Taught to recognize and respond to certain sounds such as an oven timer, an alarm clock or even a crying baby, hearing dogs are usually cross-breeds chosen for their temperament, inquisitiveness and intelligence. In the British scheme, established in 1982, all dogs used in the programme are unwanted animals, often found in dogs' homes.

A long history exists of training dogs for the relatively less useful role of entertainer and performer. In the sixteenth century dancing poodles, dressed in costume, often accompanied court jesters to entertain Queen Elizabeth I. There are stories of musical dogs, including one in Natchez, Mississippi, who could rhythmically strum a guitar with one or both paws, while the owner fingered chords on the guitar's neck. Others have been trained to yowl *somewhat* melodically when given the command 'Sing'.

Dogs can also be taught to play along with practical jokes. For instance, to circumvent No Dogs signs in hotels and trains, a British actress once trained her dog Jiggs to drape himself around her neck like a furpiece. If Jiggs became restless, she simply stroked him as women often do their stoles, though it did surprise people when one of his ears perked up or his tail flickered. At some restaurants she'd even check him in with the coats but eventually the trick became so well known that it blew Jiggs's cover!

THE INTELLIGENT DOG AND TELEPATHY

People are inclined to sneer if one claims that dogs can understand nearly every word we say . . . In fact they can understand every thought let alone words, for they have an acute telepathic sense and the spoken word becomes unnecessary.

· Barbara Woodhouse ·

Blessed with five powerful physical senses, it is widely believed that dogs also possess a sixth sense of telepathy. Certainly, the fact that some of their physical senses are so superior to ours contributes to this belief. For example, because dogs are able to isolate the sound of our approaching footsteps from hundreds of others, or identify the particular sound of our motor car, they can often tell before other household members that their owner is about to arrive. Dogs are also sensitive to changes in the environment that we aren't aware of without employing scientific instruments; often they are unsettled by an impending thunderstorm or earthquake long before it's due. (No one is sure exactly how dogs do this: whether it's an ability to detect changes in electrical or magnetic fields, or barometric pressure, or an ability to hear a wider range of sounds than we can.)

Dogs often seem to 'know' when changes are occurring *within* us too. Our moods and attitudes affect the way we smell and changes in our scent do not go unnoticed by our dog's powerful nose. A recent study suggests that some dogs could even save lives with their ability to detect when someone is about to suffer an epileptic fit or a heart attack. The study found that out of thirty-seven dogs who were with their owners when they had a seizure (none of whom were trained), all gave warnings that something was about to happen and twenty-five took decisive action during the attack, such as running for help. Attempts at faking a seizure were completely ignored by the dogs. 'Dogs are far more perceptive and sensitive of the human than they are given credit for,' writes animal researcher Andrew Edney. 'At first we thought the animals may have been picking up odours or electric changes during the process of a human epileptic seizure. But if a dog can predict a heart attack – and we believe it is possible – then the mechanism is a far more complicated one.'

Because they are keenly aware of our body language, dogs sometimes seem able to 'read our minds' and respond appropriately with a sympathetic nuzzle or knowing look in their eyes. This ability to sense what a person is feeling or thinking is well illustrated by the story of a dog named Jack. Jack's owner travelled frequently on business trips of varying lengths. His wife always knew when her husband was due home and this would invariably be confirmed by their dog. The day before his owner was due back, Jack would take his slippers and carefully place them beside his chair.

Presumably, in this instance, Jack was able to sense the wife's expectation that her husband was coming home. But there remain a number of other stories in which dogs seem to know something they could not have discovered through any of their five physical senses, powerful as these are. A sixth, telepathic sense which we do not fully understand seems to be at play.

It is well known that many dogs can tell when their owners are planning to go away or move house long before there are any signs of the forthcoming event. There are also many stories of dogs who stray or lose their owners far from home, but somehow find their way back again. In some cases dogs have been able to find their owners even when the owners have moved to a *new* home and neighbourhood – sometimes hundreds of miles away!

In 1923 a collie named Bobbie turned up again on his owners' doorstep, 2,600 miles from where he'd lost them. The family had taken Bobbie with them on a trip across the United States from their hometown in Oregon, and were filling up the car with petrol in Indiana when Bobbie wandered off and couldn't be found again. Reluctantly, the family resumed their journey without him and eventually returned home. Five months later Bobbie appeared, scratching feebly at the door and very much the worse for wear. The story was apparently authenticated through the testimony of many people who saw Bobbie on his way back.

Although collies such as Bobbie are known for their homing instinct, it is still hard to imagine how a dog could have found its way home over such a distance. 'The answer,' writes Dr Fogle, 'lies in the superlative use of the existing senses in conjunction with sensory capacities that we do not as yet fully understand.'

Even if we just consider the five senses that we *do* understand, the dog must be acknowledged as a highly intelligent and sentient being. It has a remarkable mind well-equipped to interpret signals from its environment, including some we aren't aware of. As owners, it is our responsibility to give our dogs as interesting and stimulating an existence as possible, for the more information it has to process the better its mind will function and the happier its life will be. In return we benefit from an animal that is highly trainable yet able to think for itself, ready and willing to perform for us as assistant, clever pet or hero.

III
THE DEFINITIVE
DOG I.Q. TEST

T HE FOLLOWING set of questions is designed to test your dog's I.Q. in an accurate but, above all, entertaining way. The test contains seventy questions, divided into four parts, which assess six of the seven areas of mental ability contained in I.Q. tests for humans. These include memory, reasoning ability, perception, spatial ability, vocabulary and verbal apprehension. Related areas such as imagination, curiosity and trainability are also assessed and a few questions on your dog's personality, as it reflects its intelligence, are included too.

Your dog will need to be present for thirteen of the questions which test its behaviour and response to certain situations; half of these are in Part I but the rest are interspersed throughout the test to ensure that your dog's reactions are as spontaneous and natural as possible. Most questions, however, refer to your past observations and experience of your dog.

Please select only one answer for each question. If a question does not apply or refers to an unknown situation, try to imagine how your dog would probably react and respond accordingly. Similarly, if none of the possible answers to a question applies to your dog, choose the one which best approximates to the response you would like to give.

As you respond to the questions, mark each answer for later reference to the scoring table which follows the test. After you add up the points for your dog, you can convert your dog's score into a Dog I.Q. using the graph in the Results Analysis section.

To see how your dog's I.Q. ranks among that of the domestic dog population, a percentile ranking table is also included. The domestic dog population is represented by a sample group of forty-nine dogs. At the back of the book the name, breed and sex of each dog in the sample group is given in the Sample Pool of Domestic Dogs: List of Participants.

HAVE FUN AND GOOD LUCK!

PI	PII	PIII	PIV
1 3	17 4	31 3	53 2
2 2	18 2	32 2	54 3
3 3	19 3	33 3	55 4
4 4	20 3	34 ◯	56 1
5 2	21 3	35 2	57 2
6 3	22 2	36 2	58 1
7 3	23 4	37 3	59 4
8 4	24 4	38 4	60 3
9 3	25 4	39 3	61 3
10 3	26 3	40 2	62 ◯
11 2	27 4	41 4	63 3
12 1	28 3	42 1	64 3
13 4	29 3	43 1	65 3
14 ◯	30 4	44 2	66 3
15 ◯		45 4	67 2
16 ◯	46	46 2	68 ◯
		47 ◯	69 3
34		48 3	70 4
37		49 4	
46		50 3	44
55		51 4	
44		52 3	
		55	

Part I Visual Skills

1. How does your dog react when it sees you get out its lead to take it on a walk?

   A As if it hadn't been out in months, running round in circles and not keeping still long enough to let me put the lead on. ☐

   B Very happily, wagging its tail and anxious to go. ☑

   C Nonchalantly until I actually put the lead on and we head for the door. ☐

2. When you throw a toy or object in the air for your dog to catch, how would you rate your dog's ability to judge its speed and distance?

   A Excellent. ☐

   B Good. ☑

   C Fair. ☐

[Dogs] are not as good as man at focusing on objects at close range or at judging distance . . . because of their smaller field of binocular vision.

· David Taylor, *The Ultimate Dog Book* ·

---

3. Gather up your coat and keys as if you were about to leave the house. Your dog:

   A Looks at me with a sad expression, thinking that I'm leaving. ☑

   B Looks at me with a glad expression, thinking that I'm leaving. ☐

   C Heads for the door, wanting to go out with me. ☐

   D Takes no notice. ☐

4. With your dog watching, make as if to reach for a snack and then pretend to eat it. Your dog:
   A Watches me intently as if I'm actually eating. ☐
   B Investigates the spot from which I took the 'food' ☐
      to see if anything is there.
   C Couldn't be less interested. ☐
   D Seems to realize I'm just pretending. ☑

5. There is a big fly in the house and your dog spots it. Which of the following would it probably do?
   A Nothing. ☐
   B Watch it buzz around, only trying to catch it ☑
      if it flies within easy striking distance.
   C Chase it and try to catch it in its mouth. ☐
   D Follow it and try to swat it with its paw. ☐

So have I seen ere this a silly fly
With mastiff dog in summer's heat to play,
Sometimes to sting him in his nose or eye,
Sometimes about his grisly jaws to stay,
And buzzing round about his ears to fly,
He snaps in vain, for still she whips away,
And oft so long she dallies in this sort,
Till one snap comes and marreth all her sport.

Sir John Harrington (1561?–1612),
from *The Mastiff-Worrying Fly*

---

6. Does your dog seem to realize when you're about to go on a trip?

   A Yes, once I've brought out my suitcase and begin to pack. ☑

   B Yes, even before I bring out a suitcase. ☐

   C Possibly, when I'm walking out of the door fully laden. ☐

   D No. ☐

7. Is your dog able to detect changes in your mood?

   A Yes, it is very sensitive to the way I'm feeling. ☑

   B Sometimes. ☐

   C No, not that I know of. ☐

8. If your dog was running in a park or in the countryside and its way was interrupted by a long hedgerow or fence slightly too high for it to jump over, what would it probably do?

   A Run alongside the hedgerow and look for a way around it. ☑

   B Forget about it and run off in a different direction. ☐

   C Try to burrow its way underneath or get through somehow. ☐

   D Wait for me to lift it over. ☐

9. When you look your dog in the eye and it looks
   back at you, which of the following expressions are
   you most likely to see?
   A Fevered excitement.
   B Vacancy.
   C Intelligence and understanding.
   D Aggression.

   ---

   *The gaze of dogs who don't understand and
   who don't know that they may be right not to understand.*

   · Italo Calvino (1923–85) ·

   ---

10. Look at your dog and when it looks back at you,
    smile at it. Your dog:
    A Comes over to me.
    B Does not react to my warm expression.
    C Gives a soft grunt or a warm expression in return.
    D Both A and C.

11. When your dog is on a walk, how would you rate its
    observation abilities?
    A Superb.
    B Fair.
    C Poor.

12. Your dog is facing the television screen when a commercial comes on featuring dogs. Your dog:

A Watches with interest but doesn't seem to recognize that there are dogs on the screen. ☐

B Sees the dogs and gets excited or barks. ☐

C Sees the dogs and begins to whine as if it's confused. ☐

D Is actually just staring ahead blankly in the *direction* of the screen. ☑

Dogs and cats probably see what we do on a TV screen, but whether or not their brains interpret the images as 3-D or not is unknown.

· Veterinary ophthalmologist Ken Abrams ·

13. Find a room that you can darken easily and then shut yourself and your dog inside. Switch on a torch and playfully direct the light beam around the floor. Does your dog:

A Chase the beam. ☐

B Act uninterested. ☐

C Act unimpressed but notice the dancing light. ☐

D Become curious about the torch, but not the light. ☐

E Investigate the area where the torch is shone. ☐

14. Take an unopened tin of dog food and place it in front of your dog. It:

A Recognizes the tin and gets excited. ☐

B Moves to its food bowl assuming it's about to be fed. ☐

C Doesn't seem to recognize the tin. ☐

15. Now take a piece of meat – or any other food your dog particularly likes – and dangle it in front of its nose. Then hide the food behind your back. Your dog:

A Soon loses interest, illustrating the phrase 'out of sight, out of mind'. ☐

B Looks behind my back for the food. ☐

C Stays put and/or whines, wondering where the food has gone. ☐

D Barks or growls at me, annoyed that it's being teased but doesn't look behind my back. ☐

E Sits patiently, waiting to be given the food. ☐

16. Finally, put a little of your dog's food into its bowl and just after it has started eating, interrupt it by covering the bowl with a magazine. Then lead your dog out from the room for at least five minutes. When you and your dog return to the bowl, your dog:

A Remembers there is food underneath the magazine and digs in immediately. ☐

B Investigates and sniffs the covered bowl for a minute or two before pushing the magazine aside. ☐

C Investigates and sniffs the bowl but remains perplexed. ☐

D Appears to have forgotten about the food altogether. ☐

17. Does your dog seem to recognize any of the following words (or your own variations) and, if so, how many?

    Dinner, The Vet, Bed, Goodbye

    A Yes, three or four. ☑

    B Yes, two. ☐

    C Yes, one. ☐

    D No, none. ☐

18. Your dog is sleeping peacefully when suddenly there is a loud and unusual noise from the opposite end of the house. Your dog:

    A Would spring into action immediately and quietly investigate the disturbance. ☐

    B Would lift its head and listen first for further sounds to assess whether it should get up. ☐

    C Would start to bark right away, then run to the scene. ☑

    D Would go back to sleep. ☐

19. If you are in the kitchen and begin to unwrap some food with your dog in earshot, what would it probably do?

    A Come into the kitchen as soon as it heard the sound of unwrapping. ☑

    B Come in only if it felt particularly curious or hungry. ☐

    C Not realize I was unwrapping food unless I did so right in front of it. ☐

20. When you call your dog, using its name, it:

   A Invariably responds and comes to me.

   B Always seems to recognize that its name has been called, but may or may not come.

   C Recognizes its name only occasionally.

21. If you call your dog, using a word other than its name but with the same intonation, your dog:

   A Comes as if its name has been called.

   B Seems to recognize the sound but not the word and therefore does not come.

   C Does not seem to recognize even the sound of my call.

22. If your dog is near a door and hears a strange noise outside, its *first* reaction would probably be to:

   A Begin to bark and want to go outside.

   B Ignore the noise.

   C Quietly monitor the noise.

23. Does your dog seem to realize when it is being talked about?

A Yes, and it often seems to understand the nature of the comments being made. ☑

B No, it doesn't. ☐

C Sometimes. ☐

24. How many basic dog commands, such as sit, stay, jump, lie down or paw, have you been able to get your dog to recognize and obey?

A None. ☐

B One to five. ☐

C More than five. ☑

D I haven't tried to teach it commands, but if I did my dog would learn some. ☐

E I haven't tried to teach it any but, if I did, I'd be lucky if my dog learned *one* command. ☐

25. Does your dog do any special tricks or actions on command, such as responding to: 'Find your lead', 'Bring me the ball' or 'Get in your basket'?

A Yes, several. ☑

B Yes, one or two. ☐

C No. ☐

D I haven't tried to teach it any and I doubt if it would learn any if I did. ☐

E I haven't tried to teach it any, but it would probably learn one or more if I did. ☐

26. In general, would you say your dog is a fast learner?

A No. ☐

B Not really. It usually takes a while for a message or lesson to sink in. ☐

C Yes, fairly quick. ☑

D Yes, very quick. ☐

27. How often does your dog respond to the sound of food being put in its bowl (when it's within earshot but not near enough to see what you're doing)?

A Nearly always. ☑

B Most of the time. ☐

C Some of the time. ☐

D Rarely. I usually have to call my dog to let it know there's food in its bowl. ☐

28. With your dog watching you, run a pen or pencil lightly but noisily against the side of a chair or table, making sure that your dog can't actually see what you're doing. How does your dog react to this sound?

A Captivated, remaining quite still. ☐

B It tries to attack the sound source. ☑

C It stares back at me blankly. ☐

D It registers the sound but its curiosity is not aroused. ☐

29. When your dog is looking at you, stop what you're doing and listen to an imaginary noise. Your dog:

A Enters into the spirit of the occasion by listening to the noise as well. ☑

B Exhibits little interest. ☐

C Looks confused since it can't hear any noise, perhaps whining. ☐

30. When you have your dog's attention, start to make miaowing sounds. Your dog:

A Goes wild, looking around desperately to find the cat. ☐

B Cocks its head to one side while staring at me, perplexed. ☑

C Hardly moves but growls or barks at my miaows. ☐

D Just wags its tail expectantly. ☐

E Is neither interested nor fooled. ☐

Part III Social Behaviour

31. If your dog was living in the wild in a pack, which
of the following roles would it probably assume?

A The pack leader.

B A pack follower.

C A pack follower, if not a laggard.

D My dog would probably get lost.

32. If you and your dog were in a park or in the country
and you let it off its lead for a run, which of the
following would it probably do?

A Try to lose me for ever by running into the distance
to prolong its liberty before being caught.

B Run happily for some distance, only occasionally
out of sight.

C Run happily in various directions but sticking
close to me.

*And while he follows [his Master], he sometimes runs
forward, and sometimes runs back to his Master,
and at other times plays around and wags his tail and
does everything he can to sport pleasantly with him.*

· Theodore Gaza, 15th-century Greek scholar ·

33. How does your dog feel about cats (other than any it may live with)?

A It tries to attack every one it meets. ☑

B It still approaches them naïvely and often gets scratched on the nose. ☐

C Wisely wary. ☐

D It's quite frightened of them. ☐

34. When it meets another dog in the open, your dog usually:

A Tries to play with it eagerly. ☐

B Might greet it with a sniff but is soon ready to move on. ☐

C Acts submissively. ☐

D Freezes and stares at the other dog, then tries to attack it. ☐

35. Dog vocabulary can be quite diverse and includes a number of different barks, whines, grunts, yowls and growls. Of these, how many sounds would you say your dog can make?

A Four. ☐

B Five to seven. ☑

C Eight or nine. ☐

D Ten or more. ☐

36. How do you think your dog would spend its free time if it was human?

A Organizing social events. ☐

B Playing sport. ☑

C Eating out or watching TV. ☐

D Reading books or playing with computers. ☐

37. When out on a walk, if you and your dog came across a much larger dog or even a horse, what would your dog probably do?

  A Run up and nip at the animal's feet, barking at it and harassing it. ☐

  B Growl or bark fiercely, but only from a safe distance. ☑

  C Stay out of its way. ☐

  D Approach the animal cautiously or playfully. ☐

> *. . . in the mid road he basking lay,*
> *The yelping nuisance of the way;*
> *For not a creature passed along,*
> *But had a sample of his song.*
> *Soon as the trotting steed he hears,*
> *He starts, he cocks his dapper ears;*
> *Away he scours, assaults his hoof,*
> *Now near him snarls, now barks aloof;*
> *With shrill impertinence attends,*
> *Nor leaves him till the village ends . . .*
>
> John Gay (1685–1732),
> from *The Yelping Nuisance*

---

38. When taking your dog for a walk on a lead, does it adjust its walking pace to yours?

  A Yes, most of the time. ☑

  B No. It continually strains forwards, keeping the lead so taut that its breathing becomes difficult. ☐

  C To a degree; it will run as far as it can, then double back towards me. ☐

39. If, when walking your dog on a lead, you come to a busy street, would your dog:

A Stop on the pavement, assessing whether it's safe to cross or not. ☐

B Rely on me to decide when to cross. ☑

C Continue forwards, forcing me to pull back tightly on its lead. ☐

40. If your dog's lead came loose when you were walking towards a busy road, would your dog:

A Probably run right out into the traffic. ☐

B Recognize the danger of the traffic and check before crossing. ☐

C Wait or come back to me, giving me a chance to re-attach the lead. ☑

D Probably get distracted by something along the way before reaching the busy road. ☐

41. How adept is your dog at making its own thoughts and feelings understood, through facial expressions, body language, subtle vocal messages, etc?

A Very adept. ☑

B Fairly adept. ☐

C More adept than I probably recognize. ☐

D Not very adept. ☐

42. On a walk, if your dog suddenly sees a squirrel or another small animal, what does it usually do?

A Chases it off for fun, without spending much time on it. ☐

B Pursues it earnestly, drawing upon its skills of speed and change of direction, or sneaking up on it quietly. ☐

C Starts to bark as it begins its chase, giving the animal a head start. ☑

D Lunges at the animal too eagerly and noisily to catch it. ☐

As a dog he is not clever.
To be pursued by him means, for a rabbit, everlasting life,
and, for a cat, a joke of enormous dimensions.

E. V. Lucas (1868–1938),
speaking of his black Spaniel, Shadow

43. If your dog was able to throw a dinner party for other dogs and could choose any of the following food to serve, which would be the most likely?

   A Boeuf en Croûte with a Burgundy sauce. ☐

   B Dog food. ☑

   C Roast chicken. ☐

   D Wild rabbit (that it caught itself). ☐

   E All of the above. ☐

44. When travelling in a car, your dog:

   A Won't stay still and moves from one spot to the next. ☐

   B Sits on a seat or on the floorboard, relaxed. ☑

   C Props itself up against a window, fascinated by the view. ☐

   D Flies around the car in a state of panic. ☐

45. How does your dog behave with children, other than those it may live with?

   A Aggressively. ☐

   B Playfully and kindly. ☐

   C Warily. ☐

   D Sometimes warily and sometimes kindly, depending on how the children treat it. ☑

With a child (and all children adored him) he would play by the hour, and for all his force and stature never exhibit a moment's roughness, whereas when I was engaged with him, it was like withstanding the onset of a young elephant.

H. J. Hassingham, speaking of Whiskey,
the sheepdog in *Wold Without End*

-----

46. If you are playing with your dog and decide to stop but it still wants to play, how will it let you know?
    A By whining softly. ☑
    B By trying to start the game with me again. ☐
    C By growling. ☐

47. If your dog was fed next to another dog, it would:
    A Barge over to the other dog's bowl immediately and try to eat all its food. ☐
    B Barge over to the other dog's bowl but keep a watchful eye on its own bowl at the same time. ☐
    C Not recognize this as an opportunity get more food. ☐
    D Move in on the other dog's food only after eating its own. ☐
    E Only eat its own food, as it's been trained to. ☐

48. Which of the following would your dog most likely say to a new puppy if you were to adopt one?
    A 'Hey, great! A new playmate!' ☐
    B 'My word is law around here, buddy, and don't you forget it.' ☐
    C 'You're staying *how* long?' ☑
    D 'OK, so you're cute and lovable. But I can still get attention too (I hope).' ☐

For every spoiled new-comer there is, I suppose,
throughout life an old, faithful friend who finds himself
on the shelf . . . At the beginning he had a very hard
time of it. For the puppy, chiefly by hanging on
his ear, first infuriated him into sulks, and then . . .
set to work systematically to tease and bully him.

E. V. Lucas, speaking of his dog Bush
on the arrival of a new puppy

---

49. Does your dog appear to remember people, such as
family relatives who visit only occasionally?

A No. ☐

B Yes, especially if they were friendly to my dog on
their last visit. ☑

C Sometimes. ☐

D No, but it will act as if it remembers if they offer
it some food. ☐

50. If your dog could read, which of the following
newspapers would it probably buy?

A *Daily Mail*. ☐

B *Financial Times*. ☐

C *Sun*. ☐

D *Independent*. ☑

51. When you are with your dog in the vet's waiting-
room, how does it behave?

A Apprehensively. ☑

B Wide-eyed and excited by this adventure. ☐

C Aggressively, ready to attack anything that comes
near it, especially the vet. ☐

D In a relaxed and friendly way. ☐

52

52. You and your dog are out for a walk and come across two dogs, fighting. How would your dog react?

A It would race over to join in immediately. ☐

B It would not be at all interested. ☐

C It would watch with intense interest but stay clear of the fighting dogs. ☑

D It would want to run over but only if I allowed it to. ☐

A mastiff, of true English blood,
Loved fighting better than his food.
When dogs were snarling for a bone,
He longed to make the war his own . . .

As on a time he heard from far
Two dogs engaged in noisy war,
Away he scours and lays around him,
Resolved no fray should be without him.

· John Gay from *The Meddling Mastiff* ·

Part IV Domestic Behaviour

_____

53. How would you describe your dog's guarding
abilities?

A Excellent. It is sensitive to the slightest sound yet
discerning. ☐

B Fierce and ready to attack almost anything that
moves. ☐

C Alert but wimpy. Its bark is much louder than its
bite. ☐

D As a bit of overkill. It doesn't know when to stop
barking. ☑

E Non-existent. ☐

_____

Cowardly dogs bark loudest.

John Webster (1580–1625),
from his play *The White Devil*

_____

54. When you are in the kitchen cooking, what does
your dog usually do?

A Smells the food immediately and makes a timely
appearance in the kitchen. ☐

B It will have heard me preparing before it could
have smelled anything, and it would already be
on the scene. ☐

C It wouldn't think of coming into the kitchen. ☐

D It would come in only if it was hungry. ☑

55. How does your dog behave when you sit down to a meal?

A Not very well. It's noisy, bothersome and impatient for anything I might share with it. ☐

B It sits near by patiently, knowing it has a good chance of sharing my food by behaving well. ☑

C Completely uninterested and altogether missing the opportunity for titbits. ☐

D It sits as close to me as possible, ready with a well-practised pleading expression, whine or begging position. ☐

No one taught him; but one day, the time having arrived, instead of lying down as heretofore, he erected himself, subsided on his tail, lifted his fore-paws, and was begging. Straightaway we passed utterly into his power, and he perceived it, and now in extreme cases he begs even when there is no meal in progress.

· E. V. Lucas, speaking of Boby, an Aberdeen ·

---

56. Take a piece of scrap paper and crinkle it up into a ball in front of your dog. Now toss the paper over to it. Your dog:

A Brings it back to you. ☐

B Begins to tear it into a hundred tiny bits with its teeth. ☐

C Watches it land on the floor, then just stares at it. ☑

D Swats at the paper with its paw or plays with it. ☐

E Is not interested in such a boring object. ☐

57. How curious is your dog when it's in new
    surroundings?
    A Very curious, exploring every nook and cranny. ☐
    B Reasonably curious. ☑
    C The only thing my dog is ever curious about is ☐
      what's for dinner.

58. If your dog needed a drink of water but there was
    none in its bowl it would:
    A Wait for me to notice it's empty. ☑
    B Sit next to its bowl and whine. ☐
    C Find me and begin to whine. ☐
    D Summon me to its bowl to show it's empty. ☐
    E Look for other means of refreshment such as the ☐
      toilet bowl or a puddle.

59. How does your dog behave when it's been caught
    doing something wrong and *knows* it's in trouble?
    A It looks guilty and slinks away, ears and tail ☑
      down.
    B It dashes off with a worried look in its eyes. ☐
    C It dashes off with a gleeful look in its eyes. ☐
    D It stays put but cowers in front of me. ☐

---

*The Almighty, who gave the dog to be the companion
of our pleasures and our toils, hath invested him with
a nature noble and incapable of deceit.*

· Sir Walter Scott (1771–1832) ·

---

60. Have you been able to house train your dog?

   A Yes. ☑

   B No. And I'm tempted to give up. ☐

   C More or less; my dog very rarely messes inside. ☐

[The dog] becomes housebroken not because he knows it is unnatural to perform these natural duties in the house (he never learns this) but because he knows the pain of punishment will be upon him when he does soil in certain places.

· Will Judy ·

---

61. Most dogs love to chew things. Have you been able to teach your dog what's permissible and what's not acceptable to chew in the house?

   A No. It still chews whatever it pleases. ☐

   B Yes. ☑

   C Except for a few instances, yes. ☐

62. Take out your hairdryer or another noisy electrical appliance that you use often. With your dog watching, plug it in and then wait a few seconds before turning it on. Your dog:

A Calmly leaves the room as soon as it sees the appliance. ☐

B Waits until I turn it on before walking out of the room. ☐

C Runs from the room in a panic once I've turned it on. ☐

D Stays where it is, oblivious to the noise. ☐

E Tries to attack the machine, growling or barking at it. ☐

63. How does your dog let you know when it wants to go outside or get through a closed door?

A It sits at the door and whines continuously. ☐

B It scratches gently at the door, perhaps whining a bit. ☑

C It tries to attract my attention and get me to open the door, or it opens the door itself. ☐

D It sits silently facing the shut door, waiting for it to open miraculously. ☐

64. Does your dog ever scavenge for extra food in the rubbish bin?

A No, I don't think it's ever thought of it. ☐

B No, it's been trained not to do so. ☐

C Yes, but it's so neat about it I can hardly tell when it has. ☐

D Yes, and it's extremely messy when it does. ☐

E Only if it is *very* hungry. ☑

65. You give your dog a command which it seems to understand but really does not want to obey. How many times on average would you have to issue the command before it responds?

A One more time, possibly two. ☑

B Several times, raising my voice and calling its name sternly. ☐

C Countless times. ☐

66. Many dogs have a very accurate internal body clock, knowing when their owner is due home or when it's time to be served dinner. How accurate is your dog's body clock?

A To the minute. ☐

B Fairly accurate. ☑

C I don't think my dog has one. ☐

D My schedule is too erratic for my dog to use its body clock. ☐

67. When your dog is in a playful mood, give it a toy or piece of cord to grab with its mouth and initiate a tug of war. After pulling for a while, stop as if to end the game but keep your grip. For how long does your dog maintain *its* grip?

A For less than five seconds. ☐

B For up to ten seconds, shaking the toy and/or growling to encourage me to play again. ☑

C For ten seconds or more. ☐

D Not applicable as such games just do not interest my dog. ☐

68. When a stranger visits your house, your dog:

A Barks until it sees I am in control of the situation, then quietly monitors what happens. ☐

B Barks or growls until the stranger pats it on the head. ☐

C Nips at the stranger's ankles, barks or growls, refusing to stop until the person leaves. ☐

D Greets the stranger warmly. ☐

E Barks its head off until it becomes distracted by something else. ☐

You will see in dogs a . . . quality which is perhaps the most remarkable thing about the animal . . . If he sees anybody he does not know, he shows temper, although he has not suffered in any way; but if he sees a friend, he welcomes him, even though he may never have received any kindness from him. [This] shows that he possesses a refined philosophic nature.

· Plato (427–347 BC), Book III of *The Republic* ·

---

69. If a stranger visited your house with a dog, your dog would:

A *Really* bark its head off. ☐

B Bark fiercely initially, then continue to growl for some time. ☐

C Bark or growl at first, then it might begin to play with the dog. ☑

D Want to play with the dog right away. ☐

E Immediately want to fight with the dog. ☐

> *Let dogs delight to bark and bite,*
> *For God hath made them so.*

Isaac Watts (1674–1748),
Divine Songs for Children

70. Which of the following phrases would you choose to sum up your dog's character?

A Quiet and wise. ☐

B Cunning and coy. ☑

C Sweet and clever. ☐

D Sweet but slow. ☐

E Hyperactive and thick. ☐

SCORING TABLE

Part I Visual Skills

Question 1
A = 2
B = 3
C = 1

Question 2
A = 3
B = 2
C = 1

Question 3
A = 3
B = 3
C = 4
D = 1

Question 4
A = 2
B = 3
C = 1
D = 4

Question 5
A = 1
B = 2
C = 3
D = 3

Question 6
A = 3
B = 4
C = 2
D = 1

Question 7
A = 3
B = 2
C = 1

Question 8
A = 4
B = 1
C = 2
D = 2

Question 9
A = 2
B = 1
C = 3
D = 2

Question 10
A = 3
B = 1
C = 3
D = 4

Question 11
A = 3
B = 2
C = 1

Question 12
A = 2
B = 4
C = 4
D = 1

Question 13
A = 2
B = 1
C = 2
D = 4
E = 4

Question 14
A = 3
B = 3
C = 1

Question 15
A = 1
B = 4
C = 2
D = 3
E = 4

Question 16
A = 4
B = 3
C = 2
D = 1

Part II Audio Skills

──────────

Question 17
A = 4
B = 3
C = 2
D = 1

Question 18
A = 3
B = 3
C = 2
D = 1

Question 19
A = 3
B = 3
C = 1

Question 20
A = 3
B = 3
C = 1

Question 21
A = 3
B = 4
C = 1

Question 22
A = 2
B = 1
C = 3

Question 23
A = 4
B = 1
C = 3

Question 24
A = 1
B = 3
C = 4
D = 3
E = 1

Question 25
A = 4
B = 3
C = 1
D = 1
E = 2

Question 26
A = 1
B = 2
C = 3
D = 4

Question 27
A = 4
B = 3
C = 2
D = 1

Question 28
A = 3
B = 3
C = 1
D = 2

Question 29
A = 3
B = 1
C = 3

Question 30
A = 2
B = 4
C = 3
D = 1
E = 4

Part III Social Behaviour

Question 31	Question 32	Question 33	Question 34
A = 4	A = 1	A = 3	A = 3
B = 3	B = 3	B = 1	B = 3
C = 2	C = 2	C = 3	C = 1
D = 1		D = 2	D = 1

Question 35	Question 36	Question 37	Question 38
A = 1	A = 2	A = 1	A = 4
B = 2	B = 2	B = 3	B = 1
C = 3	C = 1	C = 4	C = 4
D = 4	D = 3	D = 2	

Question 39	Question 40	Question 41	Question 42
A = 4	A = 1	A = 4	A = 3
B = 3	B = 4	B = 3	B = 4
C = 1	C = 2	C = 3	C = 1
	D = 1	D = 1	D = 2

Question 43	Question 44	Question 45	Question 46
A = 4	A = 3	A = 1	A = 2
B = 1	B = 2	B = 3	B = 3
C = 2	C = 4	C = 2	C = 1
D = 4	D = 1	D = 4	
E = 3			

Question 47	Question 48	Question 49	Question 50
A = 3	A = 1	A = 1	A = 2
B = 4	B = 2	B = 4	B = 4
C = 1	C = 3	C = 3	C = 1
D = 2	D = 3	D = 2	D = 3
E = 4			

Question 51	Question 52
A = 4	A = 2
B = 1	B = 1
C = 2	C = 3
D = 3	D = 4

Part IV Domestic Behaviour

Question 53	Question 54	Question 55	Question 56
A = 4	A = 3	A = 2	A = 4
B = 3	B = 4	B = 4	B = 2
C = 3	C = 1	C = 1	C = 1
D = 2	D = 3	D = 3	D = 3
E = 1			E = 3

Question 57	Question 58	Question 59	Question 60
A = 3	A = 1	A = 4	A = 3
B = 2	B = 2	B = 2	B = 1
C = 1	C = 3	C = 1	C = 2
	D = 4	D = 3	
	E = 4		

Question 61	Question 62	Question 63	Question 64
A = 1	A = 4	A = 2	A = 1
B = 3	B = 3	B = 3	B = 4
C = 2	C = 1	C = 4	C = 4
	D = 1	D = 1	D = 2
	E = 2		E = 3

Question 65	Question 66	Question 67	Question 68
A = 3	A = 4	A = 1	A = 4
B = 2	B = 3	B = 2	B = 2
C = 1	C = 1	C = 3	C = 3
	D = 2	D = 2	D = 2
			E = 1

Question 69	Question 70
A = 1	A = 4
B = 3	B = 4
C = 3	C = 4
D = 2	D = 1
E = 2	E = 1

RESULTS ANALYSIS
Dog I.Q. Conversion Graph

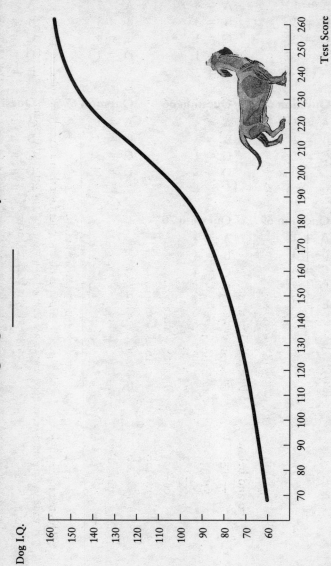

Dog I.Q.

Test Score

Dog I.Q. Percentile Ranking Table

DOG I.Q.	DOG I.Q. CATEGORY	PERCENTAGE OF DOG POPULATION MORE INTELLIGENT THAN YOUR OWN
70 and below	Blissfully Ignorant	99%
71–80	Generally Thick	92%
81–95	Occasionally Clever	85%
96–105	Average	50%
106–115	Brighter Than Average	33%
116–130	Very Intelligent	15%
131–140	Extremely Intelligent	5%
141 and above	Canine Genius	2% or less

(*Source:* Sample Pool of Domestic Dogs)

IMPORTANT MESSAGE

This test has been designed with a greater emphasis on entertainment than accuracy. Results are subject to wide variation and therefore should not be used as a basis for any personal decisions about your dog!

Don't forget to send in your results, and any Canine Genius or Blissfully Ignorant stories you may have, if you'd like to contribute to the follow-up on this book! (see pages 171–2)

IV
MAN AND DOG:
THEIR RELATIONSHIP THROUGH
THE AGES

ACCORDING TO legend, when the first man and woman appeared on earth, one of their many tasks was to assign a role to every creature in the animal kingdom. Representatives of each animal had been duly assembled when suddenly a deep chasm started to open in the ground, dividing man and woman from the beasts. Man shouted out that any animal wishing to live its life with him should leap over the quickly widening gap to join him. Only the dog had the will and the courage to make the death-defying jump, barely catching the opposite edge of the divide with its paws and then pulled to safety by man.

While the beginning of the relationship between man and dog probably wasn't quite as dramatic as this, one can *imagine* it happening because of the underlying truth in the story. Of all animals, the dog was the first to settle with man. Man's relationship with the dog was destined to become the most fruitful, multi-faceted and rewarding that he would have with any animal.

No one is exactly sure just when and how the dog came to live with man. Wild dogs probably first encountered man about ten to twelve thousand years ago, when scavenging for food at the temporary settlements man made as a nomadic hunter. If dogs found surplus food to eat there, they would surely have followed man to the next campsite, hoping to find extra food there as well. As a target himself for large animals, man had constantly to be on the lookout for possible predators, and soon would have recognized that the dog's superior sense of hearing and smell could be used to his advantage. By ensuring some food was always available for the dogs, man could rely on them to keep smaller animals at bay and away from the food, and to raise the alarm when large dangerous animals came near.

The writer John Steinbeck considered the domestication of the dog as important to the evolution of man as the discovery and use of fire: 'Through association with the dog,' he wrote, 'man doubled his perceptions, and besides this the dog – sleeping at dawn-man's feet – let him get a little rest undisturbed by creeping animals.'

After a mutual trust had been established, man and dog learned to combine their respective skills and hunt for game together. Man had his weapons, his size and a more 'user-friendly front paw', with movable thumb and fingers, and the dog had his speed, stamina and superlative senses, making them a formidable team. Together they devised new strategies for hunting, often led by the dogs who were used to living and hunting cooperatively in packs. For instance, dogs would instinctively organize group ambushes on their prey, and with man's assistance they could drive herds of panicked animals over a cliff.

Dogs soon led the way in most hunts, tracking and spotting game as they do today. Eventually, their strong hunting instinct served another useful purpose. When man progressed from his nomadic hunting lifestyle and began to keep herds and flocks of animals, he was able to draw upon this instinct to train the dog for the critical role of guardian and manager of his animals.

*The modern Border Collie, when penning sheep, shows
by the slinking gait and the fixed stare that this herding skill
derives from the instincts of a wild dog when hunting.
The final dash and the kill are absent but nearly all the other
movements of a sheepdog working sheep are also those of
a predator stalking a prey.*

· Wendy Boorer ·

The process of domesticating the dog had begun in the Middle East and by 4500 BC some of the earliest dog varieties had already been developed there through selective interbreeding. Fossils have been found of a large, Mastiff-like dog and of those resembling Greyhounds; in Ancient Egyptian paintings, two different types of Greyhounds can be seen assisting the hunt. Other breeds from this period included Sheepdogs, Pointers, the Basenji (which, uniquely, has no bark), the Saluki and Afghan, Huskies and, surprisingly, some small dogs like the Spitz.

In Ancient Egypt dogs weren't worshipped as cats were, but they were venerated throughout the country and did receive divine honours in the town of Cynopolis. We know the Egyptians considered the dog to be an important animal not only because it was featured in the paintings of royal tombs, but because if was often given a name. In Ancient Egypt, 'only a creature to whom a certain value is attached, and whose personality is recognized, is ever given a name', wrote Francis P. Cobbe. Egyptian dog names included Bahakaa and Abakaru.

As further evidence of their high regard for the dog, almost every city in Ancient Egypt had its own cemetery dedicated exclusively to the burial of dog mummies. Dogs played important roles in hunting and herding, but many were also pampered as pets. Highly decorative dog collars and bracelets made of ivory have been found there in great number.

In Ancient Persia and India, dogs were also highly valued, primarily for their obedience, companionship and guarding abilities. By 2000 BC in China dogs were already being bred for a variety of purposes including hunting, hauling, fur and meat. The Chinese were avid dog breeders and were the first to experiment in miniaturization, fostering tiny dog breeds like the ones we know today such as the Pekingese, Pug and Shih Tzu.

The only ancient civilization which didn't value dogs highly was Judaea, where dogs were mostly hated and despised. This is odd given the fact that the Jews borrowed so many cultural ideas and customs from neighbouring nations such as Egypt. They didn't dislike *all* animals, they were just generally unkind to dogs. '[But they] seem to have regarded the animal under two aspects – that of the guardian of house or herds, and of scavenger of the streets,' wrote the dog historian Edward C. Ash.

In the Bible there are thirty-six references to dogs in the canonical books, of which not a single one is favourable. For example:

they are all dumb dogs (Isaiah lvi, 10)

for they are greedy dogs which can never have enough
(Isaiah lvi, 11)

beware of dogs, beware of evil workers (Philippians iii, 2)

. . . and as if the dog were the Devil himself:

deliver . . . my darling from the power of the dog (Psalms xxii, 20)

Writings about the dog were always complimentary in Ancient Greece, however. Judging by the records and artefacts from that civilization, the dog may have been prized more highly for its character than for its utilitarian aspects. Greek philosophers especially admired dogs for the noble qualities they embodied such as fidelity, honesty and righteousness.

A dog has the soul of a philosopher.
· Plato, Book III of *The Republic* ·

Philosophers weren't the only Greeks who thought highly of dogs. Alexander the Great, founder of the Greek empire in the fourth century BC, had a dog named Peritas who went with him on a number of territorial conquests. He was so fond of the dog that he named one of the cities he captured after it.

An exemplary and noble character appears to have been of secondary importance to the Ancient Romans who valued the dog for more practical reasons, primarily as excellent hunters and guards. They were particularly impressed by the imposing Mastiff which, it is believed, they discovered in Britain, where it was brought originally by the Phoenicians. With its unusually large size and fierce nature, the Mastiff was especially well-suited to battle and to gladiatorial sport so popular at the time.

As elsewhere, some dogs were also kept as pets in the Roman Empire. A touching relic of a faithful pet dog was found in the excavations of Pompeii, the city near Naples buried in AD 79 by the eruption of a volcano. Remains of a young boy were discovered beside a large dog whose teeth were caught in the boy's coat. Apparently he had been trying to save his master from the lava and ash about to engulf them. When the silver collar around the dog's neck was polished, it showed that this wasn't the first time he had acted heroically. The inscription read: THIS DOG HAS THRICE SAVED THE LIFE OF HIS LITTLE MASTER. ONCE FROM FIRE, ONCE FROM WATER, AND ONCE FROM THIEVES.

THE DOG'S MANY ROLES
IN MYTHOLOGY AND REAL LIFE

Dogs became firmly established in most civilizations as pets, guardians, hunters and herders. As these civilizations developed, however, dogs began to serve mankind in a number of other ways.

Certain breeds which are particularly good at tracking and picking up scents, for example, were used not only in hunting, but for several centuries as assistants to search and rescue teams. Collies excel at detecting scent trails in the air, and hounds can track people lost in the wilderness by following the scent from dead skin cells (of which fifty million fall off a person every day!). One of the most famous rescue dogs was Barry, a St Bernard, who, during the early 1800s, discovered forty people lost in the snow at the notoriously perilous St Bernard's Pass in Switzerland.

I am the dog world's best detective.
My sleuthing nose is so effective.
I sniff the guilty at a distance,
And then they lead a doomed existence.
· Edward Anthony, *The Bloodhound* ·

The tracking abilities of certain breeds is also immensely helpful in the hunt for people who *don't* want to be found. A Bloodhound named Nick Carter completed more than five hundred successful trackings on the trail of criminals which resulted in hundreds of convictions. He once followed a trail that was found to be 105 hours old!

In war dogs have been employed for their powerful scenting ability, as well as for other skills. About 125 'canine soldiers' served with the U.S. troops in 1991 in Operation Desert Storm. Most were German Shepherds and Belgian Malinoises who were used to watch for intruders, be ready to attack on command and detect hidden explosives. The job required forty-five days of training for explosives detection and a further twenty-eight days of training for patrolling. Happily, all returned home safely at the end of the war.

During the Second World War, dogs were trained for a variety of tasks such as sniffing out mines and silently alerting troops when the enemy was approaching. Most dramatically, perhaps, dogs were even trained to jump out of planes with their SAS and Parachute Regiment comrades, ready to begin guard duty as soon as they hit the ground! And dogs like Beauty, a Wire-haired Terrier, rescued many people buried under the debris of bombed buildings during the Blitz in London.

There had been extensive use of dogs in the First World War as messengers, carriers of supplies across dangerous or unmanageable terrain, and as assistants in fending off rats or in laying grenades. It is estimated that seven thousand British dogs died in the line of duty during this war.

The tradition of employing dogs in war is indeed long-standing. During Ancient Roman battles, Mastiffs were often used to intimidate and attack opponents. In medieval times knights often fought with the help of their dogs, and as a testament to their importance the tombs of many knights include the representation of a dog lying at their feet.

Another critically important role of the dog has been that of hauler and carrier of goods, less glamorous perhaps than assisting soldiers or tracking criminals but one which has proved dramatic on occasion. In 1925 an Alaskan Husky named Balto led a team of dogs and one man on the final leg of a tremendously difficult 657-mile journey across Alaska to deliver medicine to a remote town whose inhabitants were suffering from a diphtheria epidemic. A blizzard had made it impossible for planes to deliver the medicine so the dogs were recruited as a last-ditch attempt. Twenty different dog teams were used, battling winds of 80 miles per hour and temperatures of −50 degrees Fahrenheit, and many lives were saved.

The dog's reputation for saving the lives of men has been embellished in mythology by a number of 'medical' superstitions. These attribute almost every part of the dog's body as a cure for one ailment or another. Some of the most unusual come from China, for example:

> The hair of the dog is used after being burnt to ashes to cure fevers, and also for the cure of a bite to [be] put on damaged tissue.

> The teeth of a dog are poisonous, but may be used by pounding into a pestle and mortar and mixed with vinegar to cure hydrophobia, also for spinal disease and sores in the thighs [if you ride your horse too long].

In parts of Great Britain an old cure for a cough required a hair from the ill person's head to be placed between two slices of buttered bread and for the sandwich to be given to the dog. Presumably it was believed that the cough would then transfer itself to the dog.

Although not fair to dogs, the idea that one's sickness could be passed on to a dog is a recurring theme in dog mythology. In several countries a charm for someone sick with fever involved pouring milk into a bowl and setting it before a dog while saying, 'Good luck, you hound! May you be sick and I be sound!' After the dog had lapped from the bowl, the ill person was supposed to take a sip, with dog and person alternating three times to ensure that the dog took the fever.

Dogs have played a mythological role as carriers of omens. According to Justus Doolittle's *Social Life of Chinese*, written in 1867, the Chinese believed that:

> ... the coming of a dog indicates future prosperity ... if a strange dog comes and remains with one, it is an omen of good to his family, indicating that he will become more wealthy. Some account for the existence of this sentiment by the remark that the dog knows beforehand where he will obtain enough to eat.

However, dogs were also perceived as omens of death in many cultures. In some areas of Wales, for instance, if a white dog was seen near the house of a dying person, it was believed that their soul would be saved after death, but if a black dog was seen their soul would suffer eternally in Hell.

Howling was often taken as an ominous sign, especially if it occurred at night. A Southern Negro myth proclaimed, 'If a dog howls twice only it foretells the death of a man, three times the death of a woman.' A Persian myth interprets howling in a less sinister way, suggesting that 'To stop a dog howling at night, turn your shoes upside-down!'

Like cats, dogs were associated with witches in the mythology of medieval Europe and were sometimes considered to be the embodiment of the devil himself. Taking the form of a black dog '. . . the dog-demon's status was higher than that of the familiar which took the shape of a cat; the latter usually remained as an inmate of the witch's house at all times, whereas the dog only appeared on special occasions, usually at the crises of the witch's career', writes Edward Ash.

Dogs are still thought to be able to take the form of ghosts. The Mauthe Dog on the Isle of Man, for example, is believed by many to haunt Peel Castle. A black Spaniel, it makes its appearances in the guard room and, according to the legend, brings a nasty and untimely death to anyone it catches drunk or misbehaving on duty. Black Shuck is another British ghost dog, with the body of a monk, the head of a dog and the shape and gait of a wolf. The word shuck comes from the Anglo-Saxon word for demon, *scucca*. A single sighting of this ghost can mean death, and it has been spotted in Suffolk, Norfolk and Cambridgeshire. Black Shuck shouldn't be mistaken for the benevolent Essex Shuck however. Although he appears as frightening as the black dog ghost, he looks after people travelling on their own in the area.

In ancient mythology the Egyptians chose the dog to represent Anubis, a jackal god associated with death, the after-life and embalming. Anubis guarded tombs and assisted Osiris's judgement of the dead, in which the heart of the deceased would be weighed against the feathers of truth and light. Dogs also featured prominently in Greek stories of the underworld. One of the most famous characters was Cerberus, a three-headed dog monster with a mane and tail made of serpents, who guarded the entrance to Hades. It was traditional for Ancient Greeks when burying their dead to include a piece of cake dipped in honey for the deceased to offer this fierce guardian.

Not all stories from ancient mythology portrayed dogs in a

bad light, though. According to one tale from Greece, the loyalty and devotion of the dog earned it a place in the heavens. The mythological figure Icarius was said to have kept a faithful dog named Maera. This dog was greatly distressed after Icarius's murder by shepherds who then threw his body down a well. Maera led Icarius's daughter, Erigone, to the well and she was so distraught that she committed suicide. The dog, equally distraught, jumped into the deep well and killed itself too. The three characters then turned into constellations in the heavens: Erigone became Virgo, Icarius became Bootes and Maera, the dog, became Canicula.

Dogs feature elsewhere in astronomical legend. The Eskimos have a touching explanation for the bright northern lights visible in their part of the world, the aurora borealis. They believe that the lights are tears shed by dogs carrying souls to heaven. The Chinese attributed solar eclipses to a celestial dog, *T'ien Kow*, thought to be eating the sun on those occasions.

One of the most intriguing superstitions from Chinese astrology is their Year of the Dog, part of a twelve-year cycle whereby each year is represented by a different animal. People born in this year are meant to share many of the same character traits as dogs, such as a desire to help and please others (especially those who are disadvantaged), loyalty, a strong work ethic and a powerful sense of justice and duty. They tend to work best in partnerships and can be idealistic in their personal life. Celebrities born in a Year of the Dog include Michael Jackson, Mother Teresa and Zsa Zsa Gabor. The next Year of the Dog starts in 1994.

In the 1950s dogs were among the first animals to participate in man's exploration of space. A Samoyed Husky bitch named Laika successfully orbited the earth in 1957 aboard Sputnik II, though sadly she died when her supply of oxygen ran out. In 1960 two Samoyed Huskies were the first animals to sur-vive being sent into space after they had travelled aboard Sputnik V.

Another recent role of the dog has been that of Hollywood film star. The most famous dog movie star was Rin Tin Tin, an Alsatian abandoned by the Germans in France in 1918 and rescued by an American army pilot. In the U.S.A., Rin Tin Tin was training with the police when his talent and looks were noticed by Warner Brothers. His first film was released in 1923 and within a few years Rin Tin Tin was one of the most popular stars in America. When he died in 1932 he had earned more than a million dollars. 'At the height of his popularity he was receiving 10,000 letters a week from devoted fans – more than Douglas Fairbanks Junior, though not as many as Mickey Mouse,' writes June Whitfield.

Lassie was the best-known stunt dog in the world and enjoyed a successful film and television career. The first Lassie was a male Collie, originally named Pal. His owner had taken him to a local dog trainer, Rudd Weatherwax, to break his habit of chasing motor cycles but, in lieu of the $75 bill, Pal was given to Weatherwax. Pal trained further and got his first film role in 1941, starring in the popular movie *Lassie, Come Home*.

Walt Disney featured many different dogs in his animated films, studying the characteristics and traits of each breed before creating his canine characters. For instance, as part of his research for the movie *One Hundred and One Dalmatians*, Disney travelled to France to observe Dalmatians – they weren't common in the States yet – and he captured their every movement and physical feature on film for his artists to reproduce. After the movie was released, the price of Dalmatian puppies in the States soared 400 per cent.

A more recent dog star, Benji, was an unlikely discovery. A director of a film company was visiting dog trainers, looking for a dog to star in his movie. He spotted one named Higgins who looked perfect for the role though he was already thirteen years old. A Poodle, Schnauzer and Cocker mix, Higgins's performance in *Benji* was named Animal Act of the Year in 1976, earning him a place in the American Humane Association's Hall of Fame.

Dogs have enriched the lives of modern man by assisting people who are physically impaired or emotionally starved. For instance, dogs are now trained as guides for the blind, signal dogs for the hearing impaired and hearing dogs for the deaf. And as participants in a programme called Therapy Dogs International, 'social' dogs pay visits to the house-bound, the elderly and hospital patients, brightening up their days by giving them something to look forward to and sometimes even reducing their pain. The Pets As Therapy (PAT) scheme in Britain has seven thousand dogs on its register. It is run by Lesley Scott-Ordish who tells the following story about her own Cocker Spaniel, Ella:

> We visited [a] little boy who was about to undergo an operation on his throat at Ipswich Hospital. He was absolutely terrified, and no amount of love and attention by staff and family could help him relax. When we walked in with Ella, he just couldn't stop himself from smiling. He began stroking the dog and had forgotten all about the operation.

Dogs are also a rewarding hobby for people who breed them, and this can become a full-time occupation. There are

now over 160 different dog breeds recognized by the Kennel Club, many of which are no more than a hundred years old. Since Victorian times dog breeders have experimented with a mixture of physical attributes of different breeds and, to a certain extent, with their character and nature.

My dog is half pit bull, half poodle.
Not much of a guard dog, but a vicious gossip.

· Craig Shoemaker ·

The earliest book on dog breeds published in England was *De canibus Britannicus* written in 1570 by Dr J. Caius. It included the first description of English breeds and, by today's standards, was an elementary exercise as Caius 'classified his various dogs into groups according to their use and nomenclature', writes Clifford L. B. Hubbard. But, he continues, 'even if this was not perhaps as scientifically correct as it might have been, it was at least more satisfying than the classification by shade of colour(!) carried out two centuries later by Pye in his *The Sportsman's Dictionary*'.

Little else was written about breeds in England again until the 1800s when people became interested in dogs generally and not only for hunting or sporting events. The first recorded dog show was organized in 1859 in Newcastle by a gunmaker, Mr Pape. Winners in this first dog show were given for prizes weapons he had made himself.

The first international dog show was in 1863 in London. Called the First Annual Grand National Exhibition of Sporting and Other Dogs, it was held in Chelsea and, though large and well-advertised, it was not an unqualified success. The show's organizer, Mr E. T. Smith, failed to recognize and provide for some of the most basic needs of the 1,200 dogs assembled there, particularly an adequate supply of water!

A writer from *Field* magazine summarized with disbelief what happened:

> ... while it is universally admitted that Mr E. T. Smith ... is a great man (in his way), it is patent to all who have witnessed his labours that he has been overwhelmed by the difficulties of the task which he has undertaken ... We should have imagined that no Englishman could be ignorant of the fact that dogs require constant access to water when in confinement; and this element is more especially necessary to their health and comfort when they are in the state of excitement inseparably connected with a dog show. An outlay of one penny per dog would have procured the 1,200 occupants ... an earthen pan which might easily have been replenished from the fountain which formed a veritable torture to Tantalus in the middle of the building ...

Today thousands of dog shows of varying size are held in countries around the world. In large shows dogs of the same breed compete against one another based on the 'standards' for their breed such as size, physique and type of coat, set by internationally recognized organizations such as the Kennel Club. 'Best of Breed' winners go on to compete against other breeds in their 'group'; dogs are divided into six groups which in Britain are defined as Working, Utility, Toy Dogs, Gun

Dogs, Hounds and Terriers. 'Best of Group' winners then compete against each other for additional prizes such as 'Best in Show'.

There are dogs you've never seen before back here.
There are dogs you've never heard of before. And there is a
certain snootiness: Pomeranians speak only to Poodles,
and Poodles only to God.

· Charles Kuralt, reporting on the Westminster Dog Show ·

THE DOG'S BIGGEST ROLE

The tradition of keeping dogs solely as pets dates back to at least six thousand years ago. In this – its biggest role – the dog continues to reign supreme in most countries. In the United States and France it is estimated that one in three families owns a dog. Pet dogs serve as companions, lapdogs or guardians of our home, and they are often considered to be fully fledged members of the family. In America over a million are said to be named as beneficiaries in the wills of their owners.

There can be few owners who have treated their pet dogs more as family members than the Eighth Earl of Bridgewater. A shoe fanatic, he had his personal shoemaker create a different pair for every day of the year and commissioned sets of leather boots for each of his many dogs. Every night he chose eleven of his dogs to join him for dinner, seated them at the table and expected them to eat from plates while listening attentively to his conversation.

In Winston Churchill's household pet dogs (as well as cats) were treated very much as part of the family. His pet poodle Rufus was allowed to sit at the table during meals and when his daughter Mary's dog, a Pug, didn't look well he wrote the following poem about it:

What is the matter with poor Puggy-wug?
Pet him and kiss him and give him a hug.
Run and fetch him a suitable drug,
Wrap him up tenderly all in a rug.
That is the way to cure Puggy-wug.

Josephine, Empress of France, also owned a Pug. Named Fortune, the dog was the source of some consternation to Napoleon on his wedding night. According to an extract in *La Vie Intime*, Napoleon pointed to the Pug, lounging on a sofa, and said to a friend, 'Do you see that gentleman; he is my rival. He was in possession of Madam's bed when I married her. I wished to remove him; it was quite useless to think of it. I was told that I must either sleep elsewhere or consent to share my bed. I gave way. The favourite was less accommodating. I bear proof on my legs of what I say.'

Other famous dog lovers have included Abraham Lincoln. A long-time friend described Lincoln in a nineteenth-century article for *The New York Times* as the 'quietest, gentlest boy' he'd ever known; he only saw him lose his temper once when Lincoln was nine years old and a drunk man kicked his dog, Honey. All Lincoln could do was '. . . jump up and down, like a girl in a tantrum, and tears ran down his face. Then he got Honey into his arms and carried him home.'

Pet dogs have captured the hearts of many royals as well. Queen Victoria kept a wide variety of dogs, perhaps after the fashion in her era for developing and acquiring new and exotic breeds. 'Her favourite was a King Charles Spaniel named Dash which she used to dress in a red jacket and blue trousers,' writes June Whitfield. 'It's said that on the day of her coronation the new queen returned from Westminster Abbey and promptly rolled up her sleeves and gave Dash a bath.'

King Edward VII had a beloved dog named Caesar, a Fox Terrier, who took pride of place at his master's funeral procession in 1910, walking just behind his master's carriage. King James I never forgave his wife for accidentally killing his dog Jewel with a crossbow while hunting. Mary, Queen of Scots was accompanied to the scaffold by her small dog, thought to be a Spaniel, whom she had hidden underneath her skirt; the dog refused to leave its mistress after the deed was done, but was later given a home with one of the queen's friends in France. Today's Queen Elizabeth II is also a well-known dog-lover whose favourite Corgi was reputedly called Susan.

Gangster is the truest friend I can ever ask for.

· Sylvester Stallone ·
speaking of his pet dog (appropriately a Boxer)

Today pet dogs are more popular than ever and with so many different breeds available to choose from, not to mention the endless variety of mixed breeds represented by mongrels, there is something for everyone in the dog world – big or small, boisterous or quiet, guard dog or lapdog. As in the many other roles we assign them, dogs readily accept the position of pet and household companion. Indeed, given the numerous ways in which they serve mankind, dogs never stop earning their well-deserved title of Man's Best Friend.

The lonely fox roams far abroad,
On secret rapine bent, and midnight fraud;
Now haunts the cliff, now traverses the lawn,
And flies the hated neighbourhood of man:

While the kind spaniel, or the faithful hound,
Likest the fox in shape and species found,
Refuses through these cliffs and lawns to roam,
Pursues the noted path, and covets home;

Does with kind joy domestic faces meet,
Take what the glutted child denies to eat,
And, dying, licks his long-loved master's feet.

The Home Loving Dog,
Matthew Prior (1664–1721)

V
THE DEFINITIVE
DOG OWNER I.Q. TEST

'I live in a lonely house and I want a good house-dog.'

'Yes, Ma'am.'

'But I don't want one that will keep me awake all night, barking at nothing.'

'No, Ma'am.'

'He must be VERY strong and VERY fierce, yet as gentle as a lamb with us, you know.'

'Yes, Ma'am.'

'He must drive EVERY tramp away that comes to the house.'

'Yes, Ma'am.'

'But, of course, he must not interfere with any HONEST person that should come along.'

'No, Ma'am.'

'If a burglar comes, the dog must attack him INSTANTLY, of course.'

'Yes, Ma'am.'

'But NOT anyone that makes a friendly call.'

'Yes, Ma'am.'

'Now, would you PLEASE show me a suitable dog?'

'Well, Ma'am, I don't suppose I've got the right sort here, Ma'am.'

'Oh, yes, I'm sure you MUST have. I'm not so particular as all that. You have got such lovely dogs. What sort would you recommend?'

'Well, Ma'am, what you wants is one of – of – these 'ere thought-readin' dogs, and I don't keep that sort.'

· Anonymous ·

———————

OWNING A DOG can bring many varied rewards including companionship, loyalty, playfulness and often humour. But being a dog owner also brings with it a number of responsibilities. To ensure that the relationship between you and your dog is a happy and successful one, you should be sensitive to its emotional needs, receptive to its attempts to communicate with you, pay regular attention to its health, put some effort into its training, reward it when it does something well and, every now and then, succumb to the charms or quirks of its personality!

The Dog Owner I.Q. Test attempts to measure your knowledge of your dog and your efforts in meeting responsibilities, as well as anything else you may do that is 'above and beyond the call of duty'. There are seventy multiple-choice questions which are divided into four sections: Background, Training, Dedication and Sensitivity.

For every question please select only one response, answering as accurately as possible. If a question does not apply to you, try to imagine which answer you would choose if the question *did* apply; if none of the possible answers applies, choose the one that is closest to the answer you would like to give.

As you take the test, mark your selections for later reference to the scoring table at the end. After adding up your points, refer to the Results Analysis section after the test to convert your score to a Dog Owner I.Q. You can then check your I.Q. against the Dog Owner I.Q. Classification Table to discover what type of owner you are – Demanding, Congenial, Doting or Sensible – and refer to the Recommended Dog Breeds section to see which type of dog might suit you best.

HAVE FUN AND GOOD LUCK!

Part I Background

1. Did you have dogs when you were growing up and, if so, how many?

   A Yes, more than three. ☐

   B Yes, one to three. ☐

   C No. ☐

   D I didn't have a dog of my own but I knew and played with other people's dogs when I could. ☐

2. Did you spend any significant time during your childhood with animals other than dogs?

   A Yes, I had a number of different pets while I was growing up. ☐

   B Yes, we had one or more cats. ☐

   C Yes, but my favourites were always dogs. ☐

   D No. ☐

3. In general, what did you think about dogs when you were growing up?

   A I considered them as friends and playmates. ☐

   B I felt neutral towards them. ☐

   C I didn't like them much. ☐

   D I liked them more than any other animal. ☐

4. How would you compare dogs with cats?

A Dogs are far friendlier, nicer, more honest and loyal than cats. ☐

B They're about the same, sometimes sweet and sometimes not. It depends on the breed and the animal's upbringing. ☐

C Dogs may be nicer, but I actually prefer cats. ☐

... Pussy will rub my knees with her head
Pretending she loves me hard;
But the very minute I go to my bed
Pussy runs out in the yard,
And there she stays till the morning-light;
So I know it is only pretend;
But Blinkie, he snores at my feet all night,
And he is my Firstest Friend!

Rudyard Kipling (1865–1936),
from *Pussy Can Sit by the Fire and Sing*

---

5. As a child, when others were unkind to a dog, how did you feel?

A Very upset. I would try to stop it if I could. ☐

B Amused. ☐

C Saddened. ☐

D I would have little or no reaction. ☐

6. When you are greeted by a dog at a friend's house, what do you usually do?

A Ask if the dog bites and/or watch with annoyance as it sniffs around my ankles. ☐

B Unless it's a particularly intimidating breed, I'll say hello and start to pat it immediately. ☐

C I might pat it on the head briefly. ☐

7. Do you think dogs make suitable pets for children?

A Yes, they can be excellent companions, teachers and guardians (except for overly aggressive dogs). ☐

B Yes, but other animals are just as suitable. ☐

C No. ☐

8. If you were to pass an attractive pet shop with time on your hands, would you:

A Go in right away and look at the puppies and other pets for sale. ☐

B Go in and see if there was anything to buy for my dog. ☐

C Probably not go in because it wouldn't interest me. ☐

9. If you were to enter a room and find an adorable puppy, would you:

A Temporarily forget what I'd come into the room for and start to play with the puppy right away. ☐

B Pat the puppy for a few minutes, then carry on with my activities. ☐

C Ignore the puppy. ☐

Master, this is Thy Servant. He is rising eight weeks old.
He is mainly Head and Tummy. His legs are uncontrolled.
But Thou hast forgiven his ugliness,
and settled him on Thy Knee . . .
Are Thou content with Thy Servant?
He is very comfy with Thee.

· Rudyard Kipling, from *His Apologies* ·

---

10. Do you believe, as some studies suggest, that keeping a dog as a pet can be beneficial to one's health?

    A Yes, absolutely. ☐

    B Perhaps. ☐

    C No, I doubt whether it makes any difference. ☐

11. How many dog-related items such as decorative accessories, ceramics, stationery and the like do you have in your home?

    A None that I can think of. ☐

    B One or two. ☐

    C Three to five. ☐

    D More than five. ☐

12. Dogs require more care and attention than other pets, especially if they're kept in the city. How do you feel about the responsibilities involved in keeping your dog?

    A I don't mind very much. My dog is worth it. ☐

    B I rarely find the responsibilities any trouble at all. ☐

    C They often feel like a burden. ☐

13. It is said that when people select a dog, they often tend to choose one which reflects aspects of their own character or self-image. Do you agree with this theory?

    A Yes. ☐

    B In some cases this might be true. ☐

    C No. ☐

14. If you had to choose one of the following qualities as the one you most appreciate in dogs, which would you select?

A Their loyalty. ☐

B Their trainability. ☐

C Their *joie de vivre*. ☐

> *Of any beast none is more faithful found,*
> *Nor yields more pastime in house, plain, or woods,*
> *Nor keeps his Master's person, or his goods,*
> *With greater care than doth the dog or hound.*

John Molle (1550–1637?),
from *The Faithfullest Beast*

Part IIa
How Well Have You Trained Your Dog?

15. How many commands have you tried to teach your dog (irrespective of the number it actually obeys)?

    A Five or more.

    B Three or four.

    C One or two.

    D None.

16. Of the commands you have tried to teach your dog, how many have you been able to get your dog to recognize and obey?

    A All of them.

    B Most of them.

    C Only one or two.

    D None.

17. How often would you say your dog does something it knows it shouldn't do?

    A Very rarely, if ever.

    B Every now and then but not often.

    C Once or twice a week perhaps.

    D Every day.

18. If caught misbehaving what does your dog usually do?

   A Carries on defiantly. ☐

   B Tries to run away. ☐

   C Stops what it's doing and cowers in front of me, ears down, looking guilty. ☐

19. With your dog close by, call it only once to come to you. Your dog:

   A Ignores me completely. ☐

   B Comes over to me slowly. ☐

   C Immediately comes to my side. ☐

20. If your dog needed to go outside to relieve itself but you weren't at home to let it out, what would it probably do?

   A Wait for me to come back and take it out (assuming I wasn't *too* long). ☐

   B Go right ahead and use somewhere inside the house, as it often does. ☐

   C Use inside, but choose the least offensive spot it can. ☐

Master, behold a Sinner!
He hath done grievous wrong.
He hath defiled thy Premises
through being kept in too long.
Wherefore his nose has been rubbed in the dirt,
and his self-respect has been bruised,
Master, pardon Thy Sinner,
and see he is properly loosed.

· Rudyard Kipling, from *His Apologies* ·

---

21. Have you been able to teach your dog not to chew or play with your possessions?

A My dog chews whatever it pleases, whenever it pleases. ☐

B In general, yes. ☐

C Yes, I've trained my dog to stay away from my things. ☐

Master – again Thy Sinner!
This that was once thy shoe,
He hath found and taken and carried aside,
as fitting matter to chew.
Now there is neither blacking nor tongue,
and the Housemaid has us in tow.
Master, remember Thy Servant is young,
and tell her to let him go!

· Rudyard Kipling, from *His Apologies* ·

22. When you throw a stick or any other object
    for your dog, what are the chances that it will
    retrieve it?

    A Slim. It usually gets distracted by something else ☐
       along the way.

    B Variable. My dog will certainly chase after it, but ☐
       may or may not bring it back to me.

    C Good. ☐

    D Excellent. ☐

    E My dog is not interested in such games. ☐

23. Your dog is with you when you are eating something
    it particularly likes. If you left the room with the
    food on the table, your dog:

    A Would move to the table immediately and help ☐
       itself.

    B Would wait patiently for my return and hope I'll ☐
       share some.

    C Would pace and sniff around the table, debating ☐
       whether to grab the food or not.

24. If you were to leave a room in the identical
    circumstances described above and your dog did not
    give in to temptation, you would:

    A Wonder if my dog was feeling all right. ☐

    B Assume my dog was not hungry. ☐

    C Reward its good behaviour with some of the ☐
       food.

25. When friends come to visit or you have a party, how does your dog behave?

A Very well. It is unobtrusive but responsive if guests wish to pet it. ☐

B Poorly. It growls menacingly and is upset at having strangers in its home. ☐

C Like a guest, mingling with the visitors and enjoying the extra attention. ☐

D As an opportunist, sniffing at unattended tabletops for food, while charming the guests for titbits as well. ☐

Part IIb
How Well Has Your Dog Trained You?

26. Do you let your dog sleep in your bed with you?
    A No. ☐
    B Yes. ☐
    C I would but it prefers its own bed. ☐

27. You've just given your dog a command, which is not terribly important, but it doesn't obey you. What would you probably do?
    A Continue issuing the command until it does obey. ☐
    B Issue the command once or twice again. ☐
    C Shrug it off. ☐
    D Think how adorable my free-spirited dog is. ☐

28. How do you feel about giving your dog food from the table?
    A I sometimes give in. ☐
    B I usually give in. ☐
    C I always give in. ☐
    D I don't give in as I think it might encourage bad behaviour.

29. If you've given your dog its usual amount of food,
    and it whines for more, do you:

    A Ignore its request because I know it's had all the ☐
       food it needs.

    B Give it as much as it wants. ☐

    C Give it a little more if I'm feeling generous. ☐

    D Wait to see if it's truly hungry or just trying its ☐
       luck.

30. What would you do if your dog caught a bad cold?

A Refer to a dog-care book or ring the vet for guidance. ☐

B Take it to the vet as soon as possible. ☐

C Wait for my dog to get better, only ringing the vet if the condition becomes serious. ☐

31. How affectionate are you with your dog?

A Very affectionate. My dog is very lovable. ☐

B Not very affectionate. ☐

C Quite affectionate. ☐

D I'd like to be more affectionate but my dog is too independent. ☐

32. How often do you let your dog get its own way, for example, by letting it sit on a forbidden chair, taking it out on an unscheduled walk, etc?

A All the time. ☐

B Quite frequently. ☐

C Every now and then. ☐

D Hardly ever. ☐

33. According to most books on dog care, approximately how many fluid ounces of water should a dog consume each day for every 20 pounds of body weight?

A 30 fl. ounces. ☐

B 13 fl. ounces. ☐

C 8 fl. ounces. ☐

34. If you see your dog chewing grass or a plant, what do you think this indicates?

    A That my dog likes greens. ☐

    B That it may not feel well and craves extra nutrients. ☐

    C That it has an appetite that will never cease to amaze me. ☐

35. How often do you find yourself sharing your thoughts with your dog?

    A Several times a day. ☐

    B Almost every day. ☐

    C Once a week or so. ☐

    D Only when I'm giving it a command or disciplining it. ☐

36. How do you usually call your dog?

    A By its name in a stern voice. ☐

    B By its name in a high-pitched or sweet voice. ☐

    C By whistling. ☐

    D By its name with my voice at its normal pitch. ☐

37. If your dog started whining to be taken for a walk, but you were engrossed in a book, what would you probably do?

    A Mark my place in the book and take the dog out. ☐

    B Continue reading until I came to the end of a chapter, then take the dog out. ☐

    C Ignore the dog unless it sounded quite desperate. ☐

38. How would you react if your dog started eating food you had prepared for a dinner party?

A I'd be furious with the dog, but more furious with myself for not putting the food out of reach. □

B I'd be annoyed but I'd realize that my dog just didn't know any better. □

C I'd be extremely irritated and would discipline my dog immediately to teach it not to do so again. □

———————

. . . With all the fury of a cook . . .
The broom-stick o'er her head she waves,
She sweats, she stamps, she puffs, she raves –
The sneaking cur before her flies;
She whistles, calls, fair speech she tries;
These nought avail. Her choler burns;
The fist and cudgel threat by turns.
With hasty stride she presses near;
He sinks aloof, and howls with fear . . .

· John Gay ·

———————

Part III Dedication

A man, his dog, his wife, came to town last Friday.
A drunken fellow jostled his wife off the side path and
stepped on one of the dog's paws. He apologized for
knocking against the wife. The man readily accepted the
apology. He then thrashed the fellow like blazes
for stepping on the dog.

· *Forest & Stream* magazine (U.S.), mid 19th century ·

---

39. How often do you go out of your way to do
    something nice for your dog?

    A Hardly ever.

    B A couple times a year.

    C Fairly often.

    D Frequently.

40. How many photographs do you have of your dog?

    A Several.

    B Several, with one or more displayed in my home
           or kept in my wallet.

    C One or two.

    D None.

41. When playing with your dog, how long does it take before you get bored?

   A Only a minute or two. ☐

   B Up to five minutes. ☐

   C Ten minutes or more as I love playing games with it. ☐

   D Not applicable as I don't play with my dog. ☐

42. How often do you walk your dog?

   A Twice a day. ☐

   B Once a day. ☐

   C Several times a day if I can. ☐

   D I don't need to as it goes out on its own quite safely. ☐

   E Although it can go out alone, I still enjoy accompanying it whenever I can. ☐

43. How often do you groom your dog (or have it groomed)?

   A Once a month or so. ☐

   B Once a week. ☐

   C Not very often because it doesn't need much grooming, but I'd do more if it was required. ☐

   D Hardly ever. ☐

44. Would you ever seriously consider taking your dog to a dog psychologist?

A Yes. ☐

B Possibly, if the problem I had with my dog was serious. ☐

C Probably not. ☐

D Absolutely not. It sounds ridiculous. ☐

45. How often do you take your dog to the vet for a check-up (excluding emergencies and other unplanned visits)?

A Once a year. ☐

B Twice a year. ☐

C I don't unless it's ill. ☐

46. After taking your dog to the vet, do you ever do something special for it?

A Yes, I like to treat it to its favourite food. ☐

B Yes, I'm extra nice to it for a day or so. ☐

C Perhaps, if the visit has been a harrowing one. ☐

D No, not really. ☐

47. Most dog-care guides suggest that owners regularly give their dogs a six-point check to help detect early signs of health problems (eyes, ears, mouth, nose, feet, paws and coat). How often do you look your dog over?

    A Never, unless it's obviously not feeling well. ☐
    B A couple of times a year. ☐
    C Once a month or so. ☐
    D Every 7–10 days on average. ☐

48. How often do you initiate playful games with your dog?

    A Several times a day. ☐
    B Once a day. ☐
    C A couple of times a week. ☐
    D A couple of times a month. ☐

49. What kind of collar does your dog wear?

    A The nicest one I could find or afford. ☐
    B One that reflects my dog's personality and looks. ☐
    C A collar that is purely functional. ☐

50. Have you given your dog an identification tag to wear on its collar?

    A Yes. ☐
    B No. ☐
    C Not yet, but I plan to. ☐

I am his Highness' dog at Kew;
Pray tell me, sir, whose dog are you?

Inscription on the collar of a dog given to the
Prince of Wales by Alexander Pope (1688–1744)

51. Do you buy your dog something special for its birthday, Christmas or other occasions?

A No. It wouldn't appreciate the significance of the gift. ☐

B Yes, I treat it as any other member of the family in this respect. ☐

C Sometimes I do. ☐

D Rarely. ☐

52. How often do you talk about your dog to other people?

A Hardly ever, unless I'm asked about it. ☐

B Every now and then, usually because the subject has arisen in the conversation anyway. ☐

C Fairly often, especially if I think they'll be interested. ☐

D Very often, whether they're interested or not. ☐

53. How do you like listening to other people tell stories about their dogs?

A I don't mind but I rarely find their stories as interesting as my own. ☐

B I quite enjoy listening. ☐

C I occasionally enjoy them, as long as they keep the stories short. ☐

D I find it unbelievably boring and remind myself not to do the same thing. ☐

54. What arrangements do you usually make for your dog when you go away for a weekend?

A I take it with me if possible, but otherwise I leave it with a friend or relative (using the kennels as a last resort). ☐

B I simply book it into a kennel. ☐

C I leave it at home and put out extra food. ☐

D I leave it at home and arrange for someone to call in to look after it. ☐

55. Do you enjoy having your dog sit on your lap or sleep by your side?

A Not especially. ☐

B Sometimes. ☐

C Most of the time. ☐

D Yes, very much. ☐

56. How would you react if your dog woke you in the middle of the night and insisted on going outside?

A I'd be extremely irritated and shoo it out of my bedroom. ☐

B I'd be irritated but might get up and let it out. ☐

C I'd be concerned and would follow my dog to see if anything was wrong. ☐

D I'd get up immediately and let my dog out for as long as it wished. ☐

A dog will stoop to any artful ruse to get his way, whimpering and jumping up and down in agony to lure an unsuspecting owner out of bed and downstairs on a frosty night, only to leave his man shivering on the back porch while he yawns and stretches his four legs and barks a couple of times at the moon.

· Corey Ford, from *Cold Noses and Warm Hearts* ·

Part IV Sensitivity

57. Understanding your dog's body language is an important part of your relationship. Which of the following best describes a dog in defensive mood?

    A Body, ears and tail held high, teeth exposed. ☐

    B Body tense, ears back, teeth exposed, tail lowered and rigid. ☐

    C Front legs down on the ground, hind legs up with back bent, tail moving back and forth, mouth open. ☐

58. Of the different types of body language given above, which one applies to playful behaviour?

    A ☐

    B ☐

    C ☐

59. How would you react if your dog accidentally broke something valuable in the house?

    A I'd be upset, but wouldn't shout at or punish my dog as it was an accident. ☐

    B I'd be furious and shout at my dog to teach it to be more careful. ☐

    C I'd be upset and shout but would regret doing so. ☐

60. How do you usually discipline your dog when it misbehaves?

   A By shouting at it. ☐

   B By berating it firmly but kindly. ☐

   C By staring it down. ☐

61. If you are particularly irritated by your dog's misbehaviour, would you ever take any of the following actions?

   1. Order it into a corner.

   2. Take away its toys.

   3. Lock it out of the room.

   4. Continue to chastise it after your initial scolding.

   A No, I would never do any of these things. ☐

   B I might do one but only in extreme circumstances. ☐

   C Yes, I'd probably do one or more. ☐

Keep in mind the awful truth that three out of four times you punish your dog, you do so unjustly for he has not been able to understand clearly what you wanted him to do.

· Will Judy ·

---

62. If you were accidentally to step on your dog, without causing it serious injury, how would you feel?

   A Not great but since it wasn't really hurt, I'd move on. ☐

   B Guilty, apologizing to it. ☐

   C Quite guilty, stroking it or offering it some food to make up. ☐

63. Your dog is unusually chatty and you suspect that it is trying to tell you something. What do you do?

A Tell it to be quiet and go away. ☐

B Ignore it. ☐

C Try to understand the message it wants to convey, making responsive sounds and following if it leads me somewhere. ☐

D Assume it just wants some attention, again. ☐

64. Do you ever think twice before disciplining your dog in front of other people?

A Sometimes but if the misdeed was serious, I'd go ahead anyway. ☐

B No. ☐

C Yes, particularly if there are other dogs around as I wouldn't want to humiliate it unnecessarily. ☐

65. Your dog has dozed off in front of the television when you decide you would like to watch a programme. Would you:

A Not turn the television on and do something else instead. ☐

B Turn it on but keep the volume down. ☐

C Go ahead and watch the programme at the usual volume. ☐

D Apologize and stroke my dog as I turn the television on. ☐

66. If you are busy and hear your dog whining in another room, do you:

A Carry on with my activities unless it sounds serious. ☐

B Go to see if it's all right. ☐

C Listen for a while to interpret the nature of the whine before getting up. ☐

67. Can you remember how your dog expresses any of the following emotions (through its barks, growls, eyes, tail, etc.)?

1. Delight or excitement.
2. Contentment.
3. Impatience.
4. Disappointment.

A Yes, I can remember all four. ☐

B Yes, three. ☐

C Yes, two. ☐

D Yes, one. ☐

E No, none. ☐

68. When you are about to sit down to a meal and your dog is watching, do you:

A Usually offer it a bit of food. ☐

B Occasionally offer it something. ☐

C Prepare a plate of *its* food, but only if it is its regular mealtime. ☐

69. What kind of sleeping arrangements have you provided for your dog (whether it uses them or not)?

A It has its own dog bed. ☐

B It has its own pillow or blanket. ☐

C I haven't made any special arrangements for it. ☐

D It has free use of anywhere in the house. ☐

70. Your dog accompanies you to the door and would obviously like to follow you outside. Which of the following are you most likely to say to your dog as you leave?

A 'Go on, get back, get out of the way . . .' ☐

B Nothing. ☐

C 'See you later.' ☐

D 'I'll be back soon and take you on a nice, long walk' (patting the dog on the head). ☐

SCORING TABLE

Part I Background

Question 1
A = 3
B = 2
C = 1
D = 2

Question 2
A = 2
B = 2
C = 3
D = 1

Question 3
A = 3
B = 2
C = 1
D = 4

Question 4
A = 4
B = 2
C = 1

Question 5
A = 4
B = 0
C = 3
D = 0

Question 6
A = 1
B = 3
C = 2

Question 7
A = 3
B = 2
C = 1

Question 8
A = 3
B = 3
C = 1

Question 9
A = 3
B = 2
C = 1

Question 10
A = 3
B = 2
C = 1

Question 11
A = 1
B = 2
C = 3
D = 4

Question 12
A = 3
B = 4
C = 1

Question 13
A = 3
B = 2
C = 1

Question 14
A = 3
B = 1
C = 3

Part IIa
How Well Have You Trained Your Dog?

Question 15
A = 4
B = 3
C = 2
D = 1

Question 16
A = 4
B = 3
C = 2
D = 1

Question 17
A = 4
B = 3
C = 2
D = 1

Question 18
A = 1
B = 2
C = 3

Question 19
A = 1
B = 2
C = 3

Question 20
A = 3
B = 1
C = 3

Question 21
A = 1
B = 3
C = 4

Question 22
A = 1
B = 2
C = 3
D = 4
E = 2

Question 23
A = 1
B = 4
C = 2

Question 24
A = 1
B = 2
C = 3

Question 25
A = 4
B = 2
C = 3
D = 1

Part IIb
How Well Has Your Dog Trained You?

————————

Question 26
A = 1
B = 3
C = 3

Question 27
A = 1
B = 4
C = 2
D = 3

Question 28
A = 2
B = 3
C = 4
D = 1

Question 29
A = 1
B = 3
C = 2
D = 4

Question 30
A = 2
B = 3
C = 1

Question 31
A = 4
B = 1
C = 3
D = 3

Question 32
A = 3
B = 2
C = 4
D = 1

Question 33
A = 0
B = 2
C = 0

Question 34
A = 1
B = 3
C = 1

Question 35
A = 4
B = 3
C = 2
D = 1

Question 36
A = 1
B = 3
C = 3
D = 1

Question 37
A = 3
B = 2
C = 1

Question 38
A = 3
B = 3
C = 1

Part III Dedication

Question 39
A = 1
B = 2
C = 3
D = 4

Question 40
A = 3
B = 4
C = 2
D = 1

Question 41
A = 2
B = 3
C = 4
D = 1

Question 42
A = 3
B = 1
C = 4
D = 2
E = 4

Question 43
A = 3
B = 4
C = 3
D = 1

Question 44
A = 4
B = 3
C = 2
D = 1

Question 45
A = 2
B = 3
C = 0

Question 46
A = 4
B = 3
C = 2
D = 1

Question 47
A = 1
B = 2
C = 3
D = 4

Question 48
A = 4
B = 3
C = 2
D = 1

Question 49
A = 3
B = 3
C = 1

Question 50
A = 3
B = 1
C = 3

Question 51
A = 1
B = 4
C = 3
D = 2

Question 52
A = 1
B = 2
C = 3
D = 4

Question 53
A = 3
B = 4
C = 2
D = 1

Question 54
A = 4
B = 2
C = 0
D = 3

Question 55
A = 1
B = 2
C = 3
D = 4

Question 56
A = 1
B = 2
C = 3
D = 4

Part IV Sensitivity
───────────

Question 57
A = 3
B = 1
C = 0

Question 58
A = 0
B = 0
C = 3

Question 59
A = 3
B = 1
C = 3

Question 60
A = 1
B = 3
C = 1

Question 61
A = 4
B = 1
C = 0

Question 62
A = 1
B = 2
C = 3

Question 63
A = 1
B = 1
C = 4
D = 2

Question 64
A = 3
B = 1
C = 4

Question 65
A = 4
B = 3
C = 1
D = 3

Question 66
A = 1
B = 3
C = 2

Question 67
A = 4
B = 3
C = 2
D = 1
E = 0

Question 68
A = 3
B = 2
C = 1

Question 69
A = 4
B = 4
C = 1
D = 3

Question 70
A = 1
B = 0
C = 3
D = 4

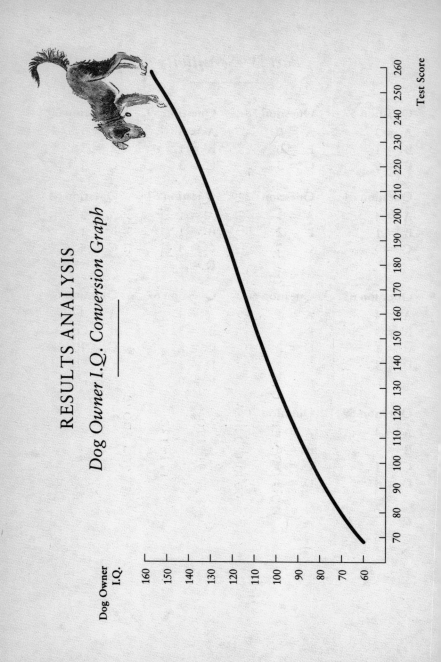

RESULTS ANALYSIS

Dog Owner I.Q. Conversion Graph

Dog Owner I.Q.

160 150 140 130 120 110 100 90 80 70 60

70 80 90 100 110 120 130 140 150 160 170 180 190 200 210 220 230 240 250 260

Test Score

Dog Owner I.Q. Classification Table

DOG OWNER I.Q.	OWNER TYPE
90 and below	Demanding
91–110	Congenial
111–130	Doting
131 and above	Sensible

RECOMMENDED DOG BREEDS
BY OWNER TYPE

Type 1: Demanding (I.Q. 90 and below)

Summary As a Demanding Owner you are best suited to dogs that are highly intelligent, easy to train and well-behaved. You probably enjoy the process of teaching your dog to work or perform for you and are especially delighted at watching your dog obey commands. Most Demanding Owners would never dream of owning a toy dog, considering them hardly dogs at all and preferring bigger breeds. You are unlikely to give your dog extra attention or rewards other than when it performs for you, and while you may appreciate limited amounts of affection you are more inclined to appreciate your dog's trainability and its loyalty to you.

Care The easier your dog is to care for the better. Ideally you can give it free access outside so that it can exercise on its own every day. Short-haired breeds are certainly preferable as you're likely to find the frequent brushing and bathing required for long-haired breeds to be a time-consuming nuisance; long dog hairs strewn around your home would also be annoying. Your perfect dog will not be too fussy about its food but content with the regular, balanced diet you have devised for it. It shouldn't nag you too often for a share of your food, either, as you would discourage such behaviour.

Features and temperament   A Demanding Owner usually prefers 'serious' dogs. Large, outdoor breeds are probably your favourite, especially those with fine features that make them excellent specimens of their breed. You are particularly well-suited to dogs that can be trained to do something useful such as retrieve or hunt. Your ideal dog will therefore be very perceptive and responsive, characteristics important in its trainability. Yet though *you* may be demanding in the standards of behaviour you set for your dog, you don't want a demanding dog. It shouldn't crave attention or want to play with you all the time. It should have a vivid imagination so that it can entertain itself.

Lifestyle and environment   Since your ideal dog is probably an active breed, independent exercise is certainly preferable. Chances are that your dog would rather chase around outside than stay indoors and have attention lavished upon it. Your ideal dog will also have a strong sense of property, making it a good watch dog. It will not be overly friendly to visitors, except those it recognizes. It will certainly consider its owner as the most important figure in its life, but will be extremely loyal to other members of the family.

RECOMMENDED DOG BREEDS

Gundogs:
Bracco Italiano
Curly Coated or Flat Coated
    Retriever
Hungarian Vizsla
Irish Water Spaniel
Large Munsterlander
Pointer
Weimaraner

Working Dogs:
Alaskan Malamute
Australian Cattle Dog
Belgian Shepherd Dog
Bernese Mountain Dog
Border Collie
Boxer
Bullmastiff
Dobermann
Estrela Mountain Dog
German Shepherd Dog
Giant Schnauzer
Great Dane
Mastiff
Pinscher
Rottweiler

Hounds:
Beagle
Borzoi
Foxhound
Greyhound
Hamilton Stovare
Ibizan Hound
Pharaoh Hound
Rhodesian Ridgeback

Utility Dogs:
Bulldog
Canaan
Japanese Akita

Terriers:
Bull
Fox (Smooth)
Irish
Welsh

Toy Dogs:
Chinese Crested Dog
English Toy Terrier
Miniature Pinscher

Type 2: Congenial (I.Q. 91 to 110)

Summary   Congenial Owners tend to be relaxed and easy-going in their relationship with their dogs. While you certainly meet all the responsibilities of caring for your dog perfectly well, you are unlikely to consider training to be of paramount importance. But you probably do not dote on your dog either. You are suited to a wide range of dogs, especially those which, like you, are happy with just a little bit of training and aren't *overly* demanding of your attention.

Care   While you are probably willing to take care of both long-haired and short-haired breeds, short-haired dogs are preferable because they need less grooming. It would be helpful if your dog can go outside on its own, so that you don't have to walk it twice a day. Chances are, though, that you enjoy walking it, just as long as it doesn't become burdensome. Your ideal dog will be happy with its own food, but it will ask every now and then to sample yours and you will usually be more than happy to agree.

Features and temperament   Small to medium-sized dogs will suit you best, though certain large breeds can also settle with you quite happily. You are likely to appreciate a dog with personality and a sweet nature. Your ideal dog will be intelligent enough to learn basic commands, though it may have an independent streak as well. It should be able to entertain itself but ideally will initiate games with you fairly often, ensuring that you're more involved with it than you might otherwise be.

Lifestyle and environment   Your ideal dog is best suited to family life which gives it many opportunities to play or to be walked when it likes. Your dog may also enjoy having another dog in the family, as playmate and companion.

RECOMMENDED DOG BREEDS

Gundogs:
Brittany Spaniel
Clumber Spaniel
Field Spaniel
Golden Retriever
Irish Red and White Setter
Labrador Retriever

Working Dogs:
Anatolian Shepherd Dog
Bouvier des Flandres
Bullmastiff
Eskimo Dog
Maremma Sheepdog
Newfoundland
Norwegian Buhund
Pinscher
Rough Collie
Siberian Husky
Smooth Collie
Swedish Vallhund
Welsh Corgi

Hounds:
Basenji
Borzoi
Deerhound

Elkhound
Finnish Spitz
Irish Wolfhound
Petit Basset Griffon
    Vendéen
Rhodesian Ridgeback
Sloughi

Utility Dogs:
Boston Terrier
Bulldog
Dalmatian
German Spitz
Keeshond
Miniature Schnauzer
Poodle
Schipperke
Shar-Pei
Tibetan Spaniel

Terriers
Bedlington
Glen of Imaal
Jack Russell
Kerry Blue
Norfolk
Norwich

Staffordshire Bull
Wire Fox

Toy Dogs:
Cavalier King Charles
   Spaniel
Chihuahua

Griffon Bruxellois
Italian Greyhound
King Charles Spaniel
Miniature Pinscher
Pug

Mongrels

Type 3: Doting (I.Q. 111 to 130)

Summary   A Doting Owner tends to think of their dog as if it were a small child and many simply can't do enough for it. Acutely sensitive to your dog's emotional and physical needs (and wishes), you are likely to be on constant stand-by, ready to pander to your dog's every whim. For this reason, you are best suited to dogs that love attention, have a challenging personality, are extremely active and require lots of grooming. Intelligence is often less important than personality and looks and, in some cases, training is unlikely to matter at all.

Care   Nothing is too much trouble for most Doting Owners if they think their dog needs or wants something. Grooming is often a delight as you are likely to find the sight of your dog with a clean, shiny and well-brushed coat very satisfying.

Long-haired breeds are sometimes preferable since they give more opportunities for grooming. Your dog probably enjoys a rich and varied diet since Doting Owners are almost always ready to share their own food. Many owners are often willing to buy different kinds of dog foods too, in case there's a new one on the market that your dog might like better.

Features and temperament   You are almost certainly suited to lively toy dogs that are attractive, manageable and enjoy being spoiled, but you might prefer a larger or more independent breed. You appreciate dogs that are excellent specimens of their breed; you may, however, be equally charmed by a particularly attractive mongrel. Depending on your lifestyle, indoor breeds that are perfectly content to lounge around and be pampered are suitable or, otherwise, highly energetic dogs that insist on playing and going out often. You may also secretly enjoy an independent dog that is playfully naughty from time to time.

Lifestyle and environment   The more people who give your dog attention the better, though it will most treasure your own signs of affection. Your ideal dog will probably choose its own favourite spots in the house to sleep, though none of these is guaranteed to be the bed you may have provided for it. Your dog may bark viciously (but without much bite) at visitors or it may be inordinately friendly, depending on its personality. Either way it will be fully prepared to call a stranger a friend as soon as the stranger demonstrates an acceptable level of adulation.

RECOMMENDED DOG BREEDS

Gun Dogs:
Cocker Spaniel
English Springer Spaniel
Golden Retriever
Irish Setter
Labrador Retriever
Welsh Springer Spaniel

Working Dogs:
Briard
Collie (Bearded or Rough)
Hungarian Puli
Komondor
Maremma Sheepdog
Mastiff
Newfoundland
Old English Sheepdog
Polish Lowland Sheepdog
Pyrenean Mountain Dog
St Bernard
Samoyed
Siberian Husky

Hounds:
Afghan
Basenji
Dachshund

Saluki
Whippet

Utility Dogs:
Chow Chow
Japanese Spitz
Lhasa Apso
Poodle
Shar-Pei

Terriers:
Border
Cairn
Dandie Dinmont
Lakeland
Norfolk
Norwich
Sealyham
Skye
West Highland White

Toy Dogs:
Affenpinscher
Australian Silky Terrier
Bichon Frisé
Chihuahua
Chinese Crested Dog

Japanese Chin
Maltese
Papillon
Pekingese
Pomeranian

Pug
Shih Tzu
Yorkshire Terrier

Mongrels

Type 4: Sensible (I.Q. 130 and above)

Summary   As their name suggests, Sensible Owners tend to have well-balanced views on dog ownership, recognizing that training is important to almost all dogs because it gives them opportunities to please their owners, but that attention is just as important. You are likely to appreciate the many benefits, both utilitarian and psychological, that come from owning a dog. You tend to take the responsibilities of dog ownership seriously and are sensitive to your dog's physical and emotional needs. While training is not the priority it is with Demanding Owners, you are not afraid to give your dog some firm handling to ensure that it is well-behaved.

Care   You are generally quite happy looking after your dog. Long-haired or short-haired breeds are equally suitable, depending largely on the time you have to groom your dog. You are also happy to accompany it on frequent walks. Even if your dog can get outside on its own, you are likely to consider it important to go with it or to play with it indoors quite regularly. With regard to your dog's diet, you are probably very responsible but not too strict. You can handle a dog with a fussy appetite since you probably share your own food with it fairly often.

Features and temperament   Sensible Owners can settle easily with a variety of dogs. Your ideal dog will want some attention from you daily and will always be responsive when you offer it your affection. A friendly, intelligent dog with a fairly lively personality will be the most communicative and rewarding pet. It should also be relatively easy to train.

Lifestyle and environment   Your ideal dog will prefer living in a family environment or alternatively in a household with many visitors. Though capable of entertaining itself, your dog will have more fun when you play with it and will appreciate most of the toys you buy for it. Outside access is preferable but not necessary as long as you give your dog good long walks every day. Indoors it will probably choose a favourite spot to call its own and it will also enjoy just being by your side.

RECOMMENDED DOG BREEDS

Gun Dogs:
Basset Griffon Vendéen
Chesapeake Bay Retriever
Cocker Spaniel
English Setter
Gordon Setter
Irish Setter
Irish Water Spaniel
Italian Spinone
Labrador Retriever
Pointer
Sussex Spaniel

Working Dogs:
Alaskan Malamute
Bearded Collie
Belgian Shepherd Dog
Bernese Mountain Dog
Bouvier des Flandres
Boxer
Dobermann
German Shepherd
Giant Schnauzer
Great Dane
Hovawart
Lancashire Heeler
Mastiff

Newfoundland
Pyrenean Mountain Dog
Rough Collie
St Bernard
Samoyed
Sheepdogs (Shetland, Old
    English, Polish Lowland)
Smooth Collie
Welsh Corgi

Hounds:
Basenji
Basset Hound
Bloodhound
Dachshund
Greyhound
Rhodesian Ridgeback
Saluki

Utility Dogs:
Bulldog (and French
    Bulldog)
Chow Chow
Dalmatian
Japanese Shiba Inu
Japanese Spitz
Keeshond

Leonberger
Lhasa Apso
Poodle
Schnauzer
Shar-Pei
Tibetan Terrier

Terriers:
Airedale
Australian
Bull
Cairn
Fox
Kerry Blue
Manchester
Scottish

Smooth Fox
Soft-Coated Wheaten
Welsh

Toy Dogs:
Australian Silky Terrier
Cavalier King Charles
  Spaniel
Italian Greyhound
King Charles Spaniel
Löwchen
Papillon
Pug
Yorkshire Terrier

Mongrels

VI
THE REWARDS
of DOG OWNERSHIP

———

———

The gift which I am sending you is called the dog, and is in fact
the most precious and valuable possession of mankind.
For while other animals are each of them of use to us in virtue
of one particular quality, and possess a special and distinguishing
excellence, this one animal is responsible for many and all kinds
of benefits to us, and is adorned with the greatest and highest
points of excellence.

Theodore Gaza, from a letter to Mohammed II
accompanying the gift of a dog

———————

WHILE THE I.Q. TESTS in this book are meant to be quite accurate, they are primarily to entertain and to offer you new insight into your dog's character and the relationship you have with your dog. Your dog's level of intelligence does of course play a part in this relationship; the more perceptive your dog is, the better it will understand your efforts to communicate with it. The stronger its memory, the more amenable it should be to training and to learning good behaviour.

But much more important is your intelligence because of the dominant role that owners have in the relationship. Dog ownership entails a certain sensitivity to your dog's needs, many of which go beyond the basic requirements of food and shelter. Owners who are 'intelligent' understand that dogs have emotional needs as well as physical ones, and that both are of equal importance to a dog's confidence, well-being and, indeed, its intelligence. In return, your dog can offer you a number of benefits, both emotional and physical. Chances are that it can also teach you meaningful lessons, some of which you may not yet have recognized.

THE INTELLIGENT DOG OWNER

There are several aspects of dog ownership that all owners should keep in mind. One of the most important is an awareness of your dog's attempts to communicate with you. Your dog will probably be trying as hard as it can to understand and please you; as a result, it is probably more sensitive to what you are saying and thinking than you are to its signals. Every dog has its own vocal language, and a dog will vary the pitch and volume of its barks or growls to communicate different thoughts. It usually does this in conjunction with body language or changes in facial expression; the thoughts and feelings of many dogs, for instance, can often be read in their eyes. By being aware of the methods your dog uses to communicate, you can recognize the messages it is trying to convey and so better understand and care for it.

Dogs laugh, but they laugh with their tails.

· Max Eastman ·

Like humans, all dogs need some attention every day. There is a direct correlation between a dog's level of interaction with its owner, other people and animals, and its level of intelligence. This factor is especially critical in the healthy development of puppies. A stimulating existence will boost a dog's spirits. Accompanying it on regular daily walks, for example, will benefit your dog who gets to exercise its body and its imagination by being out of doors, exploring new territory and scents.

Because it is so satisfying for almost all dogs to please their owner, you should give it some opportunity to do so. Train it well for, although a completely undisciplined dog may seem quite content living as a spoiled pet, a trained dog will usually be happier (as long as it has a chance to perform for you).

An animal that is properly trained,
who shares his master's work and play,
and is talked to and treated with sympathy and love,
must develop a higher intelligence and faithfulness
than one that is treated [with disregard].

· Barbara Woodhouse ·

Intelligent dog owners discipline their dogs sensibly. Many times when a dog 'misbehaves' it is because it has misunderstood what we want it to do or hasn't yet learned that its behaviour is 'bad'. You should never discipline your dog when you've lost your patience or are so angry that you've lost control. A dog should never be struck either, unless it is truly justified. Even then, one should avoid the back, ears and loins and go for the rump, preferably with a soft, rolled-up newspaper and never with anything sharp or hard. Remember though, that a tone of disappointment or a stern reproach, without any physical contact, is often all it takes to deter a dog from doing the deed again.

Lastly, be aware that as a sensitive and perceptive animal, your dog is susceptible to many of the same feelings people are, including jealousy, boredom and depression. Most dogs can also tell when they are being laughed at and this can damage their sense of pride. These emotions should be discernible in your dog's body language and expression and, on occasion, in its behaviour. So be considerate and ready to give it attention when it needs it.

Other helpful tips for the intelligent dog owner include:

- Keep a recent picture of your dog in case it gets lost or stolen
- Don't overfeed your dog and endanger its health
- Don't exercise your dog within thirty minutes after it's eaten
- Don't feed your dog anything containing small bones it could choke on
- Never beat or kick your dog as a verbal reproach is often enough to get the message across.

WHAT DOGS CAN TEACH US

Although we may have a higher intelligence than dogs, almost all of us could certainly learn a thing or two from them. The dog is a living example of a number of virtues that we might well emulate. Many of us strive to live by a few of these traits but are rarely as successful as the average dog who seems to embody them quite naturally.

One of the qualities that many adult owners could learn from is the dog's innate *joie de vivre*. Even when they're old, dogs never forget how to play, carrying the light-hearted spirits they had as puppies with them throughout their lives. And, unlike so many of us, they are always optimistic.

They are also blessed with the ability to delight in what is customary or routine. With their curiosity and remarkable use of imagination, dogs can entertain themselves for hours in the same patch of garden, discovering new scents or chasing a leaf blown by the wind. Dogs are driven by a zest for life which they apply to both familiar and new activities. They know how to live each day to its full and make the most out of every situation.

Because they apply this zeal to everything they do, dogs can concentrate for long periods. Their persistence and 'never-give-up' approach to life is legendary and has inspired many well-known phrases such as 'dog-tired', 'worked like a dog' and 'quit hounding me'.

In building their relationships with us, dogs exhibit many superior qualities. They are always ready to forgive wholeheartedly our punishments, mistakes, unfair orders and insensitivities. They don't hold grudges and they never seek revenge; instead they have a remarkable faith in humans and are always receptive when we try to make amends.

They are superior to human beings as companions. They do not quarrel or argue with you. They never talk about themselves but listen to you while you talk about yourself, and keep up an appearance of being interested in the conversation.

· Jerome K. Jerome (1859–1927) ·
from *The Idle Thoughts of an Idle Fellow*

Dogs are truly unselfish, asking for and expecting nothing. In a dog's eyes, his possessions are yours and your possessions his (sometimes quite irritating for an owner!). The strongest testament to the dog's unselfish nature is that if its owner was in danger it would not hesitate before running to help, without stopping to assess whether *its* life might be endangered or whether *it* might get hurt. Horses, cats and other animals, however, will often think twice.

Dogs are also incredibly honest. Few ever try to deceive anyone, except perhaps in a light-hearted way when playing.

---

*A man may smile and bid you hail
Yet wish you to the devil;
But when a good dog wags its tail,
You know he's on the level.*

· Anonymous ·

Dogs are able to offer their owners unconditional love, something very hard indeed to find. Jerome K. Jerome, the English novelist and playwright, equated the dog's ability to love unconditionally with an inability to discern, shown in the following passage from *The Idle Thoughts of an Idle Fellow*. He actually thought quite highly of dogs, however, and his admiration for them can be detected:

> He is very imprudent, a dog is. He never makes it his business to inquire whether you are going up or down upon life's ladder, never asks whether you are rich or poor, silly or wise, sinner or saint. You are his pal. That is enough for him, and come luck or misfortune, good repute or bad, honour or shame, he is going to stick to you, to comfort you, guard you, give his life for you, if need be – foolish, brainless, soulless dog!

Because of the strong love it has for its owner, and its desire to please, the dog is both highly prized and famous for its loyalty. Indeed, dogs are perfect examples of the word 'friend':

> I had many friends in my lifetime –
> Some who would borrow my very last dime;
> I went through life, earned what I spent.
> Paid what I owed, lost what I lent.
> My partner in business ran off with my wife,
> Then stole my child and ruined my life,
> The big bank failed where I kept my dough,
> My house burned down, I had no place to go.
> They all quit me cold when I could not lend,
> So I bought me a dog – now I have a friend.
>
> Anonymous

VIRTUOUS DOGS IN LEGEND

---

*Histories are more full of examples of the fidelity of dogs
than of friends.*

· Alexander Pope (1688–1744) ·

In 1924 in Illinois a Collie named Shep accompanied his
injured owner to St Anthony's Hospital where he was to be
treated for a fractured skull. As he was being wheeled into the
elevator, the man said, 'Wait here, Shep. I'll be back,' but sadly
he didn't survive the operation. His body was taken out of a
different part of the building, so Shep never knew what had
happened. He waited patiently for twelve years for his owner
to return, being fed and walked daily by the hospital staff, and
staunchly refusing to abandon his position. When he died a
plaque in his honour was donated by the American Humane
Association and mounted on the spot:

In fond memory of
SHEP
A Gallant Collie
Who Followed His Mortally
Injured Master into This
Hospital in 1924 and Remained
True to His Orders 'Wait Here'
Until His Own Accidental
Death in DECEMBER 1936
'His Faithful Dog Shall Bear Him Company'

A similar case occurred after the death of Warren Harding,
President of the United States from 1921 to 1923. His dog
Laddy Boy was a very playful Airedale Terrier who had full
run of the White House and often interrupted important meet-

ings in the Oval Office by insisting that the President shake his hand or throw his ball for him. Harding died on his way back from a trip to Alaska, but Laddy Boy never gave up hope that he would return and used anxiously to greet every car that arrived at the White House. When Laddy Boy died himself, school children across the nation donated their pennies in his memory and a bronze commemorative statue was built at the Smithsonian Institution in Washington, DC. It was inscribed: ON RECOGNITION BY ALL THE WORLD OF THE LOYALTY, DEVOTION AND LOVE A DOG CAN HAVE FOR HIS MASTER.

... dogges, the most faithfull and trustie companions of all others to a man.

· Pliny (translated by Philemon Halland) ·

But even when a dog *knows* its owner has died, it will often remain devoted. One of the most famous illustrations of this virtue is the story of 'The Dog of Montargis'. In early-fourteenth-century France, a nobleman was murdered by his hunting companion in the Forest of Bondi. The murderer then buried the body and fled but the grave was soon found by the nobleman's Irish Wolfhound. The dog guarded the grave until it was driven by hunger to Paris where it sought the help of a friend of his master. Led by the dog to the grave site, the friend identified the body, reported the murder and adopted the dog. At court the dog came across Macaire, the murderer, and tried to attack him. Suspicions were further roused when it was recalled that Macaire had had a heated disagreement with the nobleman shortly before the murder. Brought before King Charles VI, the dog again tried to attack Macaire and the king ordered a duel between them. The fight took place on the Ile de la Cité in Paris and attracted a large crowd. It lasted until Macaire grew too tired to fight back; the dog was just about to rip open his throat when he screamed in confession and was then escorted to be hanged. The king had a mural, featuring the duel, painted at his Montargis castle and it gave rise to the dog's special title.

The nineteenth-century English poet William Wordsworth heard a dog story which captured the romantic imagination of his era. It concerned a faithful terrier bitch who had accompanied her master, Charles Gough, on a fishing trip in early spring 1805. As they crossed over Helvellyn towards Grasmere, Gough slipped on an icy patch of rock and fell down a steep rock-face to his death. He was not discovered until three months later when a countryman heard the faint crying of the forlorn dog. Wordsworth's poem retells the story:

> A barking sound the shepherd hears,
> A cry as of a dog or fox;
> He halts – and searches with his eyes
> Among the scattered rocks:
> And now at distance can discern
> A stirring in a brake of fern;
> And instantly a dog is seen,
> Glancing through that covert green.
>
> The Dog is not of mountain breed;
> Its motions, too, are wild and shy;
> With something, as the Shepherd thinks,
> Unusual in his cry . . .
>
> Not free from boding thoughts, a while
> The Shepherd stood; then makes his way
> O'er rocks and stones; following the Dog
> As quickly as he may;
> Nor far had gone before he found
> A human skeleton on the ground;
> The appalled Discoverer with a sigh
> Looks round, to learn the history . . .

But hear a wonder, for whose sake
This lamentable tale I tell!
A lasting monument of words
This wonder merits well.
The Dog, which still was hovering nigh,
Repeating the same timid cry,
This Dog had been through three months' space
A dweller in that savage place.

Yes, proof was plain that, since that day
When this ill-fated Traveller died,
The Dog had watched about the spot,
Or by its master's side:
How nourished here through such long time
He knows, who gave that love sublime;
And gave that strength of feeling, great
Above all human estimate!

Perhaps the best-known story of a dog's fidelity and affection for its master is that of Greyfriars Bobby. In the 1850s, an Edinburgh man used to lunch with his Scotch Terrier, Bobby, at a small restaurant called Traill's Dining-rooms, near the Greyfriars churchyard. Bobby would have a bun and occasionally some scraps from the table. When the man died in 1858, he was buried in the churchyard. Three days after the funeral, Bobby appeared in the restaurant looking drawn and hungry; the proprietor, recognizing him, gave him a bun which Bobby ran off with. The next day, at the same time, Bobby reappeared and the ritual was repeated. On the third day the proprietor decided to follow Bobby who headed directly for the churchyard and his master's grave where he sat down and ate his bun.

Although he was taken home three times, Bobby always ran back to the graveyard to be by his master's side. Eventually a small shelter was built for him and for nine years he kept up the routine, collecting his bun at lunchtime and then returning to the grave. The Lord Provost of Edinburgh bought him a licence and a collar bearing the inscription: GREYFRIARS BOBBY FROM THE LORD PROVOST. 1867. LICENSED. When Bobby died in 1872 he was buried near his master.

OTHER BENEFITS OF OWNING A DOG

---

*The reward of owning a well-behaved, loving
and intelligent dog is beyond measure.
Those who have owned such a dog are truly blessed.*

· Barbara Woodhouse ·

Living with a dog can boost both your spirits and your health. According to Dr James Serpell of the School of Veterinary Medicine in Cambridge, people with pets are better able to overcome minor ailments such as headaches, colds and flu. Because stroking a dog or cat also reduces the heart rate, people susceptible to heart attacks are likely to survive longer if they have animals to pet.

Spending time with a dog can be fun, as well as relaxing and therapeutic: 'I find [they] always have a soothing effect on me.

One has to move and speak gently when one is with animals and doing that naturally makes one relax,' writes Barbara Woodhouse.

Keeping a dog also gives the satisfaction that comes from taking care of another. Recognition that there is someone in the world who depends upon you entirely and believes they couldn't exist without you can be very gratifying.

Dogs can be very valuable members of the family. They are wonderful to come home to, ready with a reliable welcome and delight at greeting you again.

In life the firmest friend.
The first to welcome, foremost to defend.

· Lord Byron (1788–1824) ·

A pet dog can also provide a good role model for children. Because the dog is dependent on the family (including children at times) for its food, water and other needs, it teaches them about responsibility. Pet dogs can serve as models of virtue and obedience, and of respect for authority; they provide a good example of how rules are applied in the household and why they should be followed. Many children also learn to appreciate the kindness in dogs, and how necessary it is in life. Indeed, reports show that children with pets in the family tend to develop better social skills than those who don't keep animals.

I think every family should have a dog; it is like having a perpetual baby; it is the plaything and crony of the whole house. It keeps them all young . . . he tells no tales, betrays no secrets, never sulks, asks no troublesome questions, never gets into debt, never coming down late for breakfast . . . is always ready for a bit of fun, lies in wait for it, and you may . . . kick him instead of someone else, who would not take it so meekly, and moreover, would certainly not, as he does, ask your pardon for being kicked.

John Brown, MD, LLD, from *Our Dogs*

THE DOG'S ONLY FAULT

The misery of keeping a dog is his dying so soon;
but to be sure if he lived for fifty years, and then died,
what would become of me?
· Sir Walter Scott ·

Dealing with the death of a beloved pet dog has never been easy. Many owners believe that their dog has a soul and upon its death wish to pay tribute to it as they would on the death of a human friend.

> I see the soul of Bunch looking out through his eyes, and I cannot draw any distinction between his soul and the human soul. I see no reason why my soul should be more immortal than his soul ... It may be that man is only a little lower than the angels and that a dog is only a little lower than man.
>
> James Douglas, from *The Bunch Book*

Today there are many ways of commemorating the life of a beloved pet dog, some more unusual than others. The Public Library of Cincinnati, for example, has started a Pet Memorial Fund whereby pet owners can donate to the Library in the name of their pet. The money raised is then used to purchase books about pets and animal care. Many pets are also named as beneficiaries in their owner's will.

Pet cemeteries can now be found in many countries, a tradition established in Ancient Egypt. And, in line with the Ancient Egyptian practice of mummifying pet animals, taxidermy is another option. In the nineteenth century it was a fashionable practice; Barry, the famous and heroic St Bernard of Switzerland, was preserved for posterity by a taxidermist in 1815. Today taxidermy is very rare but in California a few cases have recently been reported. Two Yorkshire Terriers have been deep-frozen in Los Angeles in case man one day discovers how to bring animals back to life. Even more bizarre is a Pekingese, freeze-dried in its sleeping position and placed on a coffee table in its owner's home.

All these different methods of marking the death of a pet help to overcome the sadness we feel at its departure. Rudyard Kipling accurately described this lament in his poem 'Four Feet':

> I have done mostly what most men do,
> And pushed it out of my mind;
> But I can't forget, if I wanted to,
> Four-Feet trotting behind.
>
> Day after day, the whole day through –
> Wherever my road inclined –
> Four-Feet said, 'I am coming with you!'
> And trotted along behind.
>
> Now I must go by some other round –
> Which I shall never find –
> Somewhere that does not carry the sound
> Of Four-Feet trotting behind.

The love owners have for their dogs is often expressed beautifully in the epitaphs they write for them. Some are humorous, some sombre, and many offer insight into the nature of the dog and the many pleasures of owning one. For example:

> Here rests a little dog
> Whose feet ran never faster
> Than when they took the path
> Leading to his master.
>
> Lebaron Cooke

and

Of all the dogs arrayed in fur,
Hereunder lies the truest cur.
He knew no tricks, he never flattered:
Nor those he fawned upon bespattered.

Jonathan Swift (1667–1745)

One of the most touching dog epitaphs was written by Lord Byron on the death of his Newfoundland, Boatswain, in 1808. Byron's thoughtful tribute could describe the character of all dogs, a character superior to ours in so many ways:

Near this spot
Are deposited the remains of One
Who possessed Beauty without Vanity
Strength without Insolence
Courage without Ferocity
And all the Virtues of Man without his Vices.
This praise which would be unmeaning Flattery
If inscribed over human ashes
Is but a just tribute to the Memory of Boatswain, a Dog . . .

VII
REFERENCES

Arsenis, Mylda L., *Dog Tales and Trimmings*, Howard Timmins, Cape Town, South Africa, 1957.

Ash, Edward C., *Dogs, Their History and Development*, vols 1 and 2, Ernest Benn Ltd, 1927.

Ash, Edward C., *The Practical Dog Book*, Publisher's Agents: Simpkin Marshall Ltd, 1931.

Boorer, Wendy and Woodhouse, Barbara, *The Treasury of Dogs*, Octopus Books, 1972.

Cobbe, Francis P., *The Friend of Man and His Friends, the Poets*, George Bell & Sons, 1889.

Cohen, J. M. and M. J., *The New Penguin Dictionary of Quotations*, Viking, 1992.

Dale-Green, Patricia, *Dog*, Rupert Hart-Davis Ltd, 1966.

Day, J. Wentworth, *Dog-Lover's Pocket Book*, Evans Bros Ltd, 1957.

Fogle, Bruce, *101 Questions Your Dog Would Ask Its Vet*, Michael Joseph, 1993.

Fogle, Bruce, *The Dog's Mind*, Pelham Books, 1990.

Ford, Corey (ed.), *Cold Noses and Warm Hearts*, Prentice-Hall Inc., New Jersey, 1958.

Gask, Lilian and Graham, Eleanor, *True Dog Stories*, George G. Harrap & Co. Ltd, 1950.

Green, Honor, *Just Dogs and Things*, Stanmore Press Ltd, 1964.

Hubbard, Clifford L. B., *An Introduction to the Literature of British Dogs*, published by the author at Ponterwyd, 1949.

Judy, Will, *Dog Scrap Book and Anthology*, Judy Publishing Co., Chicago, 1958.

Kennel Club, The, *The Kennel Club's Illustrated Breed Standards*, Bodley Head Ltd, 1989.

Leonard, R. Maynard, *The Dog in British Poetry*, David Nutt, London, 1893.

Lucas, E. V., *The More I See of Men . . . (Stray Essays on Dogs)*, Methuen & Co. Ltd, 1931.

Morris, Desmond, *Dogwatching*, Jonathan Cape, 1986.

New Encyclopaedia Britannica, Vol. 11, Encyclopaedia Britannica Inc., Chicago, 1988.

Oxford University Press, *The Oxford Dictionary of Quotations*, 1992.

Page-a-Day Dog Calendar, 1993, Workman Publishing Company, Inc., New York, 1992.

Pratt, A. L., *Our Friend the Dog in Verse*, Guide Dogs for the Blind Association, 1946.

Roark, Eldon, *Just a Mutt*, McGraw-Hill Book Co., 1947.

Roberts, Yvonne, *Animal Heroes*, Pelham Books, 1990.

Stampa, G. L., *In Praise of Dogs*, Frederick Muller Ltd, 1948.

Taylor, David, *The Ultimate Dog Book*, Dorling Kindersley, 1990.

White, Kay and Evans, J. M., *How to Have a Well-Mannered Dog*, Elliot Right Way Books, Surrey, 1981.

Whitfield, Judy, *Dogs' Tales*, Robson Books Ltd, 1987.

Woodhouse, Barbara, *How Your Dog Thinks*, Ringpress Books Ltd, 1992.

VIII
WHAT WERE YOUR RESULTS?

The author would like to produce a follow-up to this book which evaluates the I.Q.s of owners and their dogs by different criteria. Results will be assessed to determine, for example, whether age, sex and breed have any impact on a dog's I.Q., which dog breeds are the 'smartest' and the most popular with each owner type, and whether there is any correlation between a dog's I.Q. and that of its owner.

A collection of Canine Genius and Blissfully Ignorant dog stories will also be included. If you have a story or anecdote about your dog, which demonstrates its high level of intelligence – or lack thereof – please send it in as it could be included in the book. If so, the names of you and your dog will be kept in the story, unless you prefer to remain anonymous.

THANK YOU FOR YOUR CONTRIBUTION

Results

The Definitive Dog I.Q. Test

NAME OF DOG:

_____

AGE: SEX:

_____

BREED/DESCRIPTION:

_____

TEST SCORE: DOG I.Q.:

_____

NAME OF DOG:

_____

AGE: SEX:

_____

BREED/DESCRIPTION:

_____

TEST SCORE: DOG I.Q.:

_____

The Definitive Dog Owner I.Q. Test

NAME OF OWNER:

_____

AGE: SEX:

_____

NO. OF YEARS YOU HAVE KEPT A
DOG:

_____

TEST SCORE: OWNER I.Q.:

_____

CITY/COUNTRY:

_____

NAME OF OWNER:

_____

AGE: SEX:

_____

NO. OF YEARS YOU HAVE KEPT A
DOG:

_____

TEST SCORE: OWNER I.Q.:

_____

CITY/COUNTRY:

_____

IF YOU ARE ENCLOSING AN ANECDOTE OR STORY,
PLEASE INCLUDE YOUR ADDRESS:

_____

_____

_____

_____

Canine Genius or Blissfully Ignorant Dog Story

☐ My dog and I would like to be named in this story, if included.

☐ My dog and I would prefer to remain anonymous in this story, if included.

(PLEASE TICK THE APPROPRIATE BOX.)

_____

_____

_____

_____

_____

_____

_____

_____

_____

_____

_____

_____

_____

_____

_____

_____

_____

Please return to Melissa Miller,
The Definitive Dog I.Q. Test,
c/o Penguin Books, 27 Wrights Lane, London w8 5tz.

SAMPLE POOL OF DOMESTIC DOGS
LIST OF PARTICIPANTS

NAME OF DOG	BREED/DESCRIPTION	SEX	NAME OF OWNER	CITY/COUNTRY
Bandit	Black Labrador	M	Dominic Hawker	London
Bandit King	Shih Tzu	M	Kelly King	Naperville, Illinois, U.S.A.
Barney	Basset Hound	M	Mark Anderson	Chicago, Illinois, U.S.A.
Baudelaire	Golden Retriever	M	David M. Adams, Jr	Maisons-Laffitte, France
Bonaparte	Petit Basset Griffon Vendéen	M	Jane and Christopher Ambler	London
Buttons	Bichon Frisé	M	Linda Miller	Atlanta, Georgia, U.S.A.
Caesar	German Shepherd	M	Alex Over	Chelsfield, Kent
Cinnamon	Chow Chow	F	the Miller Family	Dallas, Texas, U.S.A.
Cleopatra	Weimaraner	F	Mr(?) Green	London
Coco (Ruweis Chanel)	Saluki	F	Mrs Karen Fisher	Chorleywood, Hertfordshire
D'Arcy (D'Artagnan)	Briard	M	the Friedman Family	Springfield, Massachusetts, U.S.A.
Davy	Pomeranian/Fawn	M	Phillis and Melodie Ho	Hong Kong
Dogges	Black Labrador	M	the Seligman Family	London
Dudley	Welsh Terrier	M	the Hodges Family	Cincinnati, Ohio, U.S.A.
Emma	Black Labrador	M	Ann Mullender	Norfolk
Fanny	Golden Retriever/ Collie Cross	F	Merrilee and Brian DeFiore	New York, N.Y., U.S.A.
Floppy	Yellow Labrador	M	Alain-Michel Habsbourg	Paris, France
Freeway	Wire Haired Fox Terrier	M	Simon Meyer	London
Gabrielle	Briard	F	the Friedmann Family	Springfield, Massachusetts, U.S.A.
Gemma	Italian Spinone	F	Marti Leimbach and Alistair Rolfe	London
Georgie	St Bernard	F	the Harris Family	Minneapolis, Minnesota, U.S.A.

NAME OF DOG	BREED/DESCRIPTION	SEX	NAME OF OWNER	CITY/COUNTRY
Gizmo	Staffordshire Bull Terrier	F	Gary Perkins	London
Harry	Cavalier King Charles Spaniel	M	the Story Family	London
Herby	Labrador/Springer	M	Lindsey Ann Miller	Tewksbury, Massachusetts, U.S.A.
Hunter	Chesapeake Bay Retriever	M	Wynn and John Henderson	Atlanta, Georgia, U.S.A.
Jake	Mongrel	M	A. Davis	New Orleans, Louisiana, U.S.A.
Jessie	Jack Russell	F	Helen and John O'Dea	London
Jimmy	Alsatian	M	Charles Miller	London
Kez	Saluki	M	Fred T. Bennett	Chorleywood, Hertfordshire
Kokomo	Boxer	F	Cheryl and Kevin Stokley	Columbus, New Jersey, U.S.A.
Mabel	Jack Russell	F	Vanessa Anderson	London
Maddie	Terrier/Poodle Mix	F	Christine and John Stark	Shaker Heights, Ohio, U.S.A.
Mozart	Mixed	M	Mary Ann Naples	Pennington, New Jersey, U.S.A.
Nutmeg	Basset Fauve de Bretagne	F	Mr and Mrs R. L. Johnson	Chorleywood, Hertfordshire
Patsy	Poodle (White)	F	E. Jackson	San Francisco, California, U.S.A.
Police Dog Acacia (Judy)	German Shepherd	F	Andrew Weaver	London
Poppy	Bulldog	F	C. J. Grievson	London
Riley	Cairn Terrier	M	Erin Koeroghlian	Austin, Texas, U.S.A.
Rocky	Rottweiler	M	Mr and Mrs M. Richards	Los Angeles, California, U.S.A.
Rolls	Terrier/Dalmatian Mix (B & W)	F	Gina Calmels	Bushey, Hertfordshire
Rosie (OcConees Rose)	Chocolate Labrador	F	Betsy Illges	Atlanta, Georgia, U.S.A.
Sam	Jack Russell Cross	M	Mr and Mrs Alexander Jones	London
Sophia Saffron Sheffawov	Pug	F	Valerie Finnis	Northamptonshire
Soufflé	Black Labrador	F	Patricia Frischer	London

NAME OF DOG	BREED/DESCRIPTION	SEX	NAME OF OWNER	CITY/COUNTRY
Tigger	Jack Russell Mix	M	Robin Aisher	Hampshire
Timothy	English Springer Spaniel (B & W)	M	N. Bromage	London
Toto	Lhasa Apso	F	L. Kirk	Houston, Texas, U.S.A.
Tuspa	Black Labrador	F	Christopher Shale	Oxfordshire
Zaki	Irish Wolfhound	M	Kelvin Vanderlip	London

SIGNET

Published or forthcoming

THE GREY HORSE

Richard Burridge

The true story of Desert Orchid

Richard Burridge was an impoverished writer when he bought a half-share in a promising grey known only as Fred in 1982. Yet for the next nine years he watched in amazement and admiration as the horse they renamed Desert Orchid galloped and jumped his way into racing legend . . .

After an early fall at Kempton Park, Desert Orchid went on to become a champion hurdler and a record four-time winner of the National Hunt Horse of the Year Award. Right up until his retirement in 1991, 'Dessie' captured the hearts of the British public with his jumping, his enthusiasm and his courage.

The story of Desert Orchid is a fairy tale come true. *The Grey Horse* is that story. The full dramatic account of the life and times of Britain's favourite racehorse, as told by one of the people who knew and loved him best.

SIGNET

Published or forthcoming

BEACHES

Iris Rainer Dart

Once in a lifetime you make a friendship that lasts forever ...

From the moment Cee Cee Bloom and Bertie Barron collide on the beach at Atlantic City aged ten and seven, they are friends ... for life. In time Cee Cee, a talented singer and comedienne, successfully pursues Hollywood stardom, while Bertie chooses the conventional life of marriage and motherhood. But despite the striking differences between them, the two women sustain each other through thirty years of careers and children, jealousy and drugs, lovers and divorce. And when they are torn apart by a shattering tragedy, against all odds Cee Cee and Bertie find strength in their extraordinary friendship.

'Well-written, well-constructed and thoroughly enjoyable' – *Daily Telegraph*

SIGNET

Published or forthcoming

A MATTER OF FAT

Sherry Ashworth

Eating is sexy, sensual, wonderful, indulgent – how could they resist temptation . . .

At the Heyside branch of Slim-Plicity the women are valiantly struggling with their waistbands while waiting for the spare flesh to melt away. Stella, their mentor, is so proud of them – they are going to be the slimmest group in the north-west, and qualify for the celebration buffet. Meanwhile, in a nearby meeting room, the unabashed members of the Fat Women's Support Group virtuously agree that dieting is a tool of women's oppression used by men and the media to torment the overweight . . .

'In *A Matter of Fat*, Ashworth has retained a wicked sense of humour, while raising some very important questions. Does she have the answers, though? You'll have to read the book if you want to find out!' – *New Woman*

SIGNET

Published or forthcoming

DEFINITIVE I.Q. TEST FOR CATS
and
I.Q. TEST FOR CAT OWNERS

Melissa Miller

A brand new edition of the accurate, entertaining assessment of your cat's brainpower.

When your cat is wearing an expression of mystic beauty, is it contemplating the meaning of life, or just wondering what's for dinner? When it winds itself round your legs does it simply want another saucer of milk? And how suitable an owner are you? Do you toss and turn, disturbing puss's valuable beauty sleep? Are you suitably grateful when your cat drops small, dead rodents at your feet? Is your cat an Einstein of the feline world?

FIND OUT IN THIS IRRESISTIBLE, ORIGINAL CAT I.Q. TEST

Four tests for your cat and four for you so that you can check your mutual compatibility or choose a suitable breed of cat for your way of life. Packed with historical and mythological references, literary quotations and a whole new section of reader's humorous anecdotes, this book is a must for all cat owners, potential cat owners and felines everywhere.